Low-Cost, High-Interest Programming

Seasonal Events for Preschoolers

Gail Benton and *Trisha Waichulaitis*

Neal-Schuman Publishers, Inc.
New York   London

Published by Neal-Schuman Publishers, Inc.
100 William Street, Suite 2004
New York, NY 10038

Printed and bound in the United States of America

The paper used in this publication meets the minimum requirements of American National Standard for Information Sciences—Permanence of Paper for Printed Library Materials. ANSI Z39.48-1992.
∞

Library of Congress Cataloging-in-Publication Data

Benton, Gail, 1950–
Low-cost, high-interest programming : seasonal events for preschoolers / Gail Benton, Trisha Waichulaitis.
     p. cm.
  Includes bibliographical references and index.
  ISBN 1-55570-502-2 (alk. paper)
    1. Children's libraries—Activity programs. 2. Education, Preschool—Activity programs. I. Waichulaitis, Trisha, 1954- II. Title.

Z718.1.B47 2004
372.5—dc22
                           2004047434

This book is dedicated to our families.

Gail

In loving memory of my mom who's career was devoted to the education of children; to my children Kristy, A. J., and Jessica, and my grandchildren Cody, Sydney, and Zane, for loving the childlike qualities in me.

Trisha

To mom and dad for instilling an "I can do it" attitude; to my husband (and personal computer tech) Pete, for his undying love while running paperclip, glue, and whiteout errands; to my son Stephen for helping mom "get the beat," and to his wife Julia for providing me with my biggest "little" fan—three-year-old granddaughter, Bethany.

Contents

Seasonal Program 1: Teddy Bear Picnic 1

Children celebrate their favorite stuffed animal as they play the Teddy Bear way.

Seasonal Program 2: Winterfest 57

Children celebrate this season with heartwarming stories and winter fun.

Seasonal Program 3: Spring Fling 123

Children blossom as they celebrate the joys of spring through stories and crafts.

Seasonal Program 4: Halloween Boo **187**

Children celebrate Halloween with a costume parade and treats.

List of Figures

Seasonal Program 1: Teddy Bear Picnic

Seasonal Program 2: Winterfest

Seasonal Program 3: Spring Fling

Seasonal Program 4: Halloween Boo

Preface

Low-Cost, High-Interest Programming: Seasonal Events for Preschoolers contains fun-filled, innovative, preschool programs—complete from start to finish—that can be presented easily and economically. These educational and entertaining programs feature over 70 activities that school and public librarians, preschool and elementary teachers, daycare providers, and recreational directors can use to bring children and caregivers together in a playful environment. Parents and children will enjoy an interactive experience while participating in fun activities like singing songs, making crafts, and listening to stories. These events create lasting effects far beyond the preschool years.

Fun Topics

Fill thirty minutes or an afternoon with engaging activities! Each unit in this book contains multiple, thematically related components that generate endless possibilities. The crafts, storytimes, fingerplays, games, and other activities work well either individually orcombined together into a smaller series or staged as special events in their entirety. The ready-to-use materials allow each event to be created and implemented immediately, reducing the time busy professionals spend researching and developing programs.

Teddy Bear Picnic: Bring your teddy bears for fun inside or out as toddlers fish in the fishing hole, pick berries, practice their bear crawl, or enter the cave of a snoring bear. Delightful activities are designed to incorporate fine and gross motor skills in a country fair atmosphere.

Winterfest: Warm a traditional winter night—wherever you are located—as families gather together to play snowball toss, try their luck at ice fishing, and share stories. Adults are encouraged to reveal their child-like enthusiasm and model good sportsmanship as they celebrate the wonders of winter.

Spring Fling: Celebrate spring with imaginative stories, songs, and craft activities! These crafts are designed to ensure a child's individual success, while allowing them their own artistic style. So put on your visors and grab your sunglasses. It's time to bloom!

Halloween Boo: Get ready for some not-so-scary stories or maybe just go trick-or-treating. Children will gather dancing jack-o-lanterns, cat masks, and other friendly, Halloween treats, while parading to the "Halloween March," in a safe environment.

Fun Materials

The programs—and their individual parts—may be used in random order, so that each of the seasonal programs offers core elements to help guide facilitators and ease planning. The programs begin with a unique title, overview description, and a detailed outline of the event. They feature a program flyer for publicizing the event, a certificate of participation—perfect for parents and caregivers—and step-by-step instructions. Station signs identify each activity and keep your participants on course and organized. Patterns, directions, and illustrations in recipe-like formats assist in creating each fingerplay, story, craft, and game. For your guests, there are activity sheets with printed instructions.

The accompanying enhanced CD-ROM contains all of the materials and handouts, reproducible in full-size PDF formats. The CD-ROM allows you to replicate publicity pages, map illustrations, certificates, bookmarks, or individual activity cards. With real size patterns for flannel, magnetic, and prop story presentations, preparation will be a breeze. The audio portion, which can be played on boom boxes, stereos, or your computer's media player, offers eight tracks, including, a chant called "The Teddy Bear Romp," a sound effect of "Snoring Bear," and the story of "Little Rabbit and the Vegetable Garden." Songs include: "Snowflake Song," "Build a Snowman," "Butterfly! Butterfly!" "One Dark and Gloomy Night," and "The Halloween March."

We developed *Low-Cost, High-Interest Programming* to expand traditional preschool programs in a unique and stimulating way. This fresh new approach encourages active play, social behavior, and interactive communication. It brings children and their caregivers together in fun and learning. More importantly, it presents an opportunity for parents to emulate these pleasant interactions that research indicates is an important role in early childhood brain development.

Low-Cost, High-Interest Programming has evolved from our work in presenting successful programs to our youngest patrons and their parents. Our activities contribute to a more sound foundation for learning by introducing children to books and libraries. They also play an important part in emergent literacy, strengthen parent-child relationships, and promote children's literature. *Low-Cost, High-Interest Programming* achieves this goal by taking advantage of a child's natural curiosity and fun-loving spirit. We have the opportunity to provide positive first experiences that incorporate fun and learning for little ones. It is our hope that you will enjoy hosting these programs as much as your audience will enjoy attending them.

Acknowledgments

Our special thanks to: Vickie Hoff and Stephen Waichulaitis for arranging and playing the musical scores, Marcus Howard for narrating our story "Little Rabbit and the Vegetable Garden," and to Vickie and Marcus for "singing along."

Teddy Bear Picnic

Description

Celebrate every child's favorite stuffed animal by inviting children and their parents and caregivers to this festival of teddy bear activities. Hold your Teddy Bear Picnic on the lawn or in a nearby park if weather allows. A large room is also suitable for this activity. Invite parents to bring a picnic lunch to enjoy with their family. If you choose to provide drinks and treats, this information should be included in your advertisement. To prepare for the Teddy Bear Picnic, line up several volunteers to assist with "stations." Each station is an independent activity for the child to enjoy. The volunteer or staff member assisting maintains order, and places a stamp or sticker on "activity cards" as each activity is completed. An activity card pattern, certificate of participation, instructions to set up stations, and story scripts and patterns are included for planning your Teddy Bear Picnic.

Publicity Page

Ready-to-personalize flyers are provided to make advertising your program a snap. To personalize, use the CD ROM or simply cut and paste your program information onto the master and then reproduce. Enlarge and color your flyer to create an eye-catching poster for display.

(see Figure 1.1 on page 14)

Certificate

Easy-to-make certificates are wonderful keepsakes for parents and caregivers. Certificates may be handed out at the conclusion of your program (best for small crowds) or simply placed at one of the stations for parents and caregivers to help themselves.

To create certificates, you will need enough paper so that each participant receives one.

To Make Certificates:

1. Use CD ROM and print, type, or cut and paste your library name, logo, date, library director's or mayor's signature, or other information onto certificate pattern.
2. Copy enough certificates—one for each child.

(see Figure 1.2 on page 15)

Bookmark

A whimsical bookmark to color may be reproduced and given at any time during your program. You may also choose to distribute the bookmark prior to your event, along with the publicity flyer, as a form of advertisement.

(see Figure 1.3 on page 16)

Activity Card

An activity card, worn around each participant's neck, provides a record of stations completed and adds excitement to the event. As a child finishes a station, a small sticker or stamp is placed in the corresponding space. Activity cards are certainly optional, but will help to ensure that every child is able to have a turn at each station. This is also a great way to count attendance—limit treats to one per child and encourage children to move along from station to station. If time and resources allow, encourage children to repeat their favorite stations without receiving an extra sticker or stamp.

To create activity cards, you will need the following items:

* card stock (enough to reproduce one card for each participant)
* yarn (cut into 30-inch lengths—one length per card)

   NOTE: Be sure stickers or stamps fit in spaces provided on activity card. Activity cards should be available at all stations so that children can start at any station.

To Make Activity Cards:

1. Reproduce pattern on card stock—one card for each participant.
2. Hole punch top center of each card as marked.
3. Thread yarn through the hole and tie ends. (To keep yarn from tangling, after tying, wrap yarn around finger and tape to back of card with removable tape.)

   (see Figure 1.4 on page 17)

Map

Create a map of your station layout. This will help volunteers locate their station and also help you decide how many chairs and tables you will need. Remember to include directions to the nearest restrooms, drinking fountains, lost and found, and first aid station, so volunteers can refer to the map to direct participants. This is also a great place to add a checklist. Be sure to give each volunteer stickers or stamps, activity cards, a bottle of water, etc. A sample map is provided as a guide.

(see Figure 1.5 on page 18)

Station Signs

Station signs identify activities in which children and their parents and caregivers may participate. To create station signs you will need the following items:

* twenty pieces of paper or cardstock
* crayons or markers

- laminate or clear contact paper (enough to cover signs)
- tape
- ten stakes or poles
- hammer

To Make Signs:

1. Reproduce two signs for each station.
2. Color signs.
3. Laminate or cover signs with clear contact paper.
4. Tape each set of station signs back to back, leaving a 4-inch opening in the bottom middle of each sign.
5. Hammer stake or pole into ground at each station location.
6. Slide sign over stake or pole.

   NOTE: Laminated signs may be used year after year.

   (see Figures 1.6, 1.7, 1.8, 1.9, 1.10. 1.11, 1.12, 1.13, 1.14, 1.15 on pages 19 to 28)

Activities

The following activities are provided for you:

- The Bear Crawl *(on page 3)*
- Bear Tales *(on page 3)*
- Bear's Cave *(on page 9)*
- Beary Yummy Treats *(on page 10)*
- The Berry Patch *(on page 10)*
- Creative Paws *(on page 10)*
- The Fishing Hole *(on page 11)*
- Hoop the Honeycomb *(on page 12)*
- Hungry Bear *(on page 12)*
- Toss the Bug *(on page 13)*

The Bear Crawl

A tunnel for little bears to crawl through is an activity, which can be run by a volunteer who has limited mobility. Plastic crawl tunnels are placed end to end for little ones to crawl through. If plastic tunnels can't be acquired, large refrigerator boxes make a perfect substitution. When a child finishes at this station, be sure to praise them and then place a sticker or stamp in the corresponding space on their activity card.

Bear Tales

Here are some stories that can be enjoyed by children of all ages. No sticker or stamp is given at this station. If children leave before a story has concluded, passing out stickers would be too disruptive to the storyteller.

To create this station, you will need several stories, a storyteller, and a cozy location. Choose or let the storyteller choose a few short stories to repeat throughout the entire event.

Stories

The following stories and patterns are provided for you:
- Bear's Wonderful Day *(on pages 4 to 5)*
- Four Little Apples *(on page 5)*
- Little Ants *(on pages 6 to 7)*
- The Teddy Bear Romp *(on page 7)*
- Where Is the Picnic? *(on pages 7 to 9)*

Bear's Wonderful Day

(Before you begin, place "party rock" behind the largest rock, and then place the other rocks randomly on the flannel board.)

Bear woke up early and yawned, stretched, and jumped out of bed.

(Place Bear on board.)

He brushed his teeth, then set off down the road. He knew it was going to be a wonderful day.

Soon Bear saw Badger.

(Place Badger on board next to Bear.)

Badger was carrying something. When Badger saw Bear, he quickly waddled behind a big rock.

(Place Badger under one of the rocks.)

Bear felt a little sad because Badger didn't even say hi. But Bear didn't let it bother him because he knew it was going to be a wonderful day.

Next Bear saw Rabbit.

(Place Rabbit on board next to Bear.)

Rabbit was carrying something. When Rabbit saw Bear, he quickly hopped behind a big rock.

(Place Rabbit behind a different rock.)

Bear felt sad because Rabbit didn't even say hi. But Bear didn't let it bother him because he knew it was going to be a wonderful day.

Then Bear saw Squirrel.

(Place Squirrel on board next to Bear.)

Squirrel was carrying something. When Squirrel saw Bear, he quickly scampered behind a big rock.

(Place Squirrel behind a different rock.)

Bear felt very sad because Squirrel didn't even say hi. But Bear didn't let it bother him because he knew it was going to be a wonderful day.

Just then Bear saw Skunk.

(Place Skunk on board next to Bear.)

Skunk was carrying something. When Skunk saw Bear, he quickly disappeared behind a big rock.

(Place Skunk behind a different rock.)

Bear felt so very sad and when he went home. Mama was waiting for him.

"Mama, why are all of my friends hiding from me?" Bear asked.

"Hmmmm," said Mama. "Why don't you go and see?"

So Bear ran all the way back to the big rock...

(Place Bear next to the big rock.)

and he peeked behind it.

(Remove big rock to reveal the "party.")

"SURPRISE!" "HAPPY BIRTHDAY, BEAR!" they all yelled at once.

Bear smiled and said, "I knew it was going to be a wonderful day!"

To Make as a Magnetic Story:

1. Reproduce patterns.
2. Color all patterns in colors of your choice.
3. Laminate patterns.
4. Cut out pieces.
5. Attach a magnetic strip to the back of each piece.

    (see Figures 1.16, 1.17, 1.18, 1.19, 1.20, 1.21, 1.22, 1.23 on pages 29 to 36)

Four Little Apples

(Before beginning, place the tree with four apples on it on the flannel or magnetic board.)
Four little apples hanging on a tree,
   (Point to the apples as you count them.)
The wind blew hard, and now there are three.
   (Make wind noise by blowing, then remove one apple from tree.)
Three little apples a worm began to chew,
   (Make chewing noise.)
Another apple hit the ground,
   (Clap.)
and now there are two.
   (Remove another apple.)
Two little apples hanging in the sun,
   (Shade eyes with hand.)
Along came a hungry Bear, and now there is one.
   (Remove another apple.)
One little apple left upon the tree,
   (Point to apple.)
I saw it before it was gone,
   (Point to self.)
I guess this one belongs to me!
   (Remove last apple and pretend to eat.)

To Make as a Flannel Story:

1. Cut all patterns from felt colors of your choice.
2. Enhance with felt markers.

    (see Figures 1.24, 1.25, 1.26 on pages 37 to 39)

To Make as a Magnetic Story:

1. Reproduce patterns.
2. Color all patterns in colors of your choice.
3. Laminate patterns.
4. Cut out pieces.
5. Attach a magnetic strip to the back of each piece.

    (see Figures 1.24, 1.25, 1.26 on pages 37 to 39)

Little Ants

One little ant climbs up the hill,
  (Place one ant on top edge of flannel board.)
Where do you think he will go?
Two little ants walking along,
  (Place second ant behind first ant.)
Looking for food, don't you know?
Three little ants all in a line,
  (Place third ant behind second ant.)
Searching up high and down low.
Four little ants busy at work,
  (Place fourth ant behind third ant.)
  Marching along in a row.
Five little ants spy a fine treat,
  (Place fifth ant behind ant.)
Lifting it with a heave-ho.
  (Place plastic vegetable on top of all five ants.)
Bringing the food back to their friends.
  (Carefully lift vegetable with ants attached.)
HEY! Watch out below!
  (Tip vegetable and disappear behind flannel board.)

To Make as a Prop Story:

You will need to create five ants. To create ants you will need the following supplies:

- one strip of self-adhesive black Velcro (twelve inches)
- five black pompoms (3/4-inch)
- ten black pompoms (1/2-inch)
- ten jiggly eyes (1/8-inch)
- twenty old-fashioned hairpins
- hot glue gun
- glue sticks

To Make Ant:

1. Hot glue the two 1/2-inch pompoms together (for head and thorax).
2. Hot glue the 3/4-inch pompom in line with the other two. (This will create the ant's body.)
3. Open three hairpins and reshape each one into an "M."
4. Hot glue hairpins to pompoms to resemble legs.
5. Cut 1/2 inch off open end of last hairpin. (The newly-created pieces will be used to resemble antenna.)
6. Glue antenna into place on top of ant's head.

7. Glue eyes in place.
8. Repeat above steps to make four more ants.
9. Cut a 6-inch piece of Velcro into small pieces and attach one side of the piece to the top of each ant.
10. Discard opposite pieces of Velcro.
11. Purchase any plastic vegetable approximately 6-8 inches in length (e.g., carrot, celery).
12. Separate remaining 6-inch strip of Velcro.
13. Use side that will stick to the pieces attached to the ants and glue along the length of the plastic vegetable.

(see Figure 1.27 on page 40)

The Teddy Bear Romp

(Have children join you, following this simple chant's directions. Play number one from CD.)
Teddy bears, stand up let's go!
It's time for us to do a show.
Clap your hands now, one, two, three,
Clap once more and pat your knee.
Jump up high and jump down low,
Turn around very slow.
March, march, march and stomp, stomp, stomp.
We just did the Teddy Bear Romp!

Where Is the Picnic?

(Before beginning, place all items out of sight.)
Here is the picnic the ants ate.
(Place picnic basket on table.)
Here is the cloth
that was placed on the ground
for the picnic the ants ate.
(Shake cloth and then place on table next to picnic basket, and hold up picnic basket.)
Here is the dog
which lay on the cloth
that was placed on the ground
for the picnic the ants ate.
(Bark, then place dog on the table next to the cloth, shake cloth, and hold up picnic basket.)
Here is the Frisbee
that was thrown for the dog
which lay on the cloth
that was placed on the ground
for the picnic the ants ate.

(Place Frisbee on table next to the dog, then hold up dog, bark, shake cloth, and hold up picnic basket.)

Here is the boy
who brought the Frisbee
that was thrown for the dog
which lay on the cloth
that was placed on the ground
for the picnic the ants ate.

(Place cap on your own head, then place on table next to the Frisbee, hold up Frisbee, hold up dog, bark, shake cloth, and hold up picnic basket.)

Here is the mom
who drove the boy
who brought the Frisbee
that was thrown for the dog
which lay on the cloth
that was placed on the ground
for the picnic the ants ate.

(Put lipstick on own lips, put cap on own head, hold up Frisbee, hold up dog, bark, shake cloth, and hold up picnic basket.)

Here is the dad
who married the mom
who drove the boy
who brought the Frisbee
that was thrown for the dog
which lay on the cloth
that was placed on the ground
for the picnic the ants ate.

(Place mustache under own nose, then take it off and place it on the table next to the tube of lipstick, put lipstick on own lips, then lay tube on table next to the cap, put cap on own head, hold up Frisbee, hold up dog, bark, shake cloth, and hold up picnic basket.)

Here is the sandwich
that went in the picnic
that was made by the dad
who married the mom
who drove the boy
who brought the Frisbee
that was thrown for the dog
which lay on the cloth
that was placed on the ground
for the picnic the ants ate.

(Put sandwich in the picnic basket, then place basket back on table, place mustache under own nose, then take it off and place it on the table next to the tube of lipstick, put lipstick on own lips. Then lay

tube on table next to the cap, put cap on own head, hold up Frisbee, hold up dog, bark, shake cloth, and hold up picnic basket. Place hats on heads, pick up picnic basket, and say:)

And here are the aunts! "We ate the picnic!"

> NOTE: It's best if you can have a guest to help you with the surprise ending of this story. If you are going to be telling the story alone, simply substitute the word "ant" for "ants" throughout the story and change the last line to "Hi, I'm the aunt, and I ate the picnic!"

To Make as a Prop Story:

You will need to gather the following items:

- one piece of brown felt (1/8-inch)
- double stick tape for mustache (see Figure 1.28)
- picnic basket (any type)
- small tablecloth (or material to resemble a tablecloth)
- stuffed dog (or puppet)
- Frisbee
- baseball cap
- tube of dark lipstick (preferably red)
- felt sandwich (or purchase plastic pet sandwich)
- white glue
- two hats (the wilder the better)

To Make Mustache:

1. Cut pattern from brown felt.
2. Attach double stick tape to one side of mustache.

   (see Figure 1.28 on page 41)

To Make Felt Sandwich:

1. Cut patterns from felt colors as marked.
2. Glue "peanut butter" and "jam" between two white "bread" pieces.
3. Let glue dry.

   (see Figure 1.29 on page 42)

The Bear's Cave

This cave is home to a sleeping bear. Shhh!—don't wake him up. Children love to sneak into the Bear's Cave to have a look!

To create this activity, you will need the following items:

- one large refrigerator (or stove) box
- large brown tarp (sheet or piece of material)
- CD player
- large stuffed bear

1. Place the box on its side and drape with tarp (sheet or piece of material), slightly covering entrance.
2. Place stuffed bear at far end of box.
3. Place CD player on top of box, hidden under tarp (sheet or piece of material).
4. Play number 2 "Snoring Bear" from CD and watch the fun!

When a child finishes at this station, be sure to acknowledge their bravery and then place a sticker or stamp in the corresponding space on their activity card.

Beary Yummy Treats

Hungry "Bears" can find sweet treats at this station. Many local retailers or fast food chains are willing to donate treats in exchange for advertisement at your event. Goodies can be limited to children only—this will cut the number of items required. Remember to provide napkins. When a child receives their treat, be sure to place a sticker or stamp in the corresponding space on their activity card.

The Berry Patch

Children love collecting colorful berries at this "berry" simple station. A volunteer that has limited mobility can easily run this berry picking activity.

To create this activity, you will need the following items:

- twenty hedge balls of each color: blue (blueberries), purple (boysenberries), red (raspberries), and pink (strawberries)
- six to eight plastic buckets (or make your own using empty plastic containers with braided yarn handles—if possible, buckets and/or handles should match the berry colors)

1. Mix all the "berries" together and toss them randomly onto the ground.
2. When signal is given, have children gather berries and place them in their basket. (Younger children can pick up any berry they choose. Older children can be directed to pick up only the berries that match their bucket or handle color.)

When a child finishes at this station, have them return buckets filled with berries to the volunteer, who will then toss them again for the next crowd of anxious children. Be sure to praise their efforts and then place a sticker or stamp in the corresponding space on their activity card.

Creative Paws

Young and old alike love craft projects. This station offers an opportunity for parents and caregivers to work with their children, creating a simple craft to take home.

To create this station, you will need two or three tables covered with disposable plastic tablecloths or butcher paper. Provide all supplies needed for the craft you have selected. Several craft ideas with patterns and directions on each page are provided. When a child finishes at this station, be sure to praise their efforts and then place a sticker or stamp in the corresponding space on their activity card.

The following craft patterns with instructions are provided for you:

- Balloon Bookmark Craft
  (see Figure 1.30 on page 43)
- Bee Hive Craft
  (see Figures 1.31, 1.32 on pages 44 to 45)

- Brady Bear Craft

  (see Figure 1.33 on page 46)
- Dress the Bear Craft

  (see Figure 1.34, 1.35 on pagse 47 to 48)
- Panda Mask Craft

  (see Figure 1.36 on page 49)

The Fishing Hole

The "catch and release" fishing hole is always a hit. Fish are placed into the fishing hole and several children attempt to "catch" fish at the same time. A paper clip is attached to each fish's mouth. Poles are equipped with magnets at the end of a cotton string. To create a fishing hole with fish and poles, for fifteen participants at a time, you will need the following items:

- wooden dowels (18-inch lengths—one for each fishing pole)
- cotton string (24 inches per pole)
- roll of self-adhesive magnetic strip (1/2 inch per pole)
- large blue plastic tarp or paper for fishing hole
- eight to ten rocks to hold tarp or paper in place
- variety of colored paper to reproduce approximately one hundred fish from patterns
- small paper clips (one per fish)

To Make Fishing Hole:

- Place tarp on the ground, tucking ends under to create a rounded look for the fishing hole, and secure with rocks. If using paper, cut into an interesting rounded shape and secure with rocks.

To Make Fish:

1. Reproduce fish from patterns *(Figures 1.37, 1.38 on pages 50 to 51)* using colored paper. (Use both fish patterns to reproduce fish back to back on same piece of paper, creating a front and back to each fish.)
2. Place paper clip on the mouth of each fish.

   OPTIONAL: Provide enough fish for each child to take one or two home.

To Make Fishing Pole:

1. Drill a hole at one end of each dowel—large enough to thread string through.
2. Thread a 24-inch piece of cotton string through each hole and tie knot.
3. Stick a 1/2-inch piece of self adhesive magnet to loose end of each string. (Be sure to cover entire sticky side of magnet with string.)
4. To avoid tangles, when not in use, wrap string around each pole.

Place fish in fishing hole. Let children have fun "catching" and then releasing several fish. Restock as needed. When a child finishes at this station, be sure to praise their efforts and then place a sticker or stamp in the corresponding space on their activity card.

Hoop the Honeycomb

Let each "little bear" try their luck ringing hoops around a honeycomb.
To create this activity, you will need the following items:

- two packages of 9-inch disposable plastic plates (any color)
- ten empty 2-liter pop bottles with lids
- twenty pieces of 8 1/2 x 11-inch yellow paper
- laminate or clear contact paper (enough to cover yellow paper)

To Make Hoops:

- Cut the center out of each plate, leaving a 2-inch edge.

To Make the Honeycombs:

1. Using yellow paper, copy twenty honeycomb patterns. (Two will be used for each pop bottle.)
2. Laminate or cover patterns with clear contact paper.
3. Fill 2-liter bottles with water and replace lid. (This will keep bottle from tipping over.)
4. Tape two honeycomb papers together along 11-inch sides. Wrap around bottle, covering bottle, then secure with tape.
5. Place the honeycombs on ground in a random pattern at least two feet apart.

Encourage children to participate by tossing one hoop at a time, trying to ring a honeycomb. Let children stand a comfortable distance from any of the honeycombs (let child determine this distance), and take several turns tossing the hoops. When a child finishes at this station, be sure to praise their efforts and then place a sticker or stamp in the corresponding space on their activity card.

(see Figure 1.39 on page 52)

Hungry Bear

Feeding a bear seems endless. Children will love the challenge of tossing beanbags into the tummy of a bear, hoping to fill him up!
To create this activity, you will need the following items:

- one paint stick
- one empty cardboard box without lid
- two brown paper bags
- two pieces of 8 1/2 x 11-inch brown paper
- laminate or clear contact paper (enough to cover brown paper)
- two dozen beanbags

(If beanbags are not available, fill balloons or colored socks with dried beans or rice.)

To Make the Bear:

1. Copy the bear head and feet patterns onto 8 1/2 x 11-inch brown paper.
2. Cut out patterns.
3. Laminate or cover patterns with clear contact paper.

4. Cover box using brown paper bags (writing side in).
5. Attach the bear head to the paint stick.
6. Attach the paint stick to the upper inside edge of the cardboard box. (Bear should be facing into the box.)
7. Attach feet to opposite end of box.

Children toss beanbags into the box to feed the bear. When a child finishes at this station, be sure to praise their efforts and then place a sticker or stamp in the corresponding space on their activity card.

(see Figures 1.40, 1.41 on pages 53 to 54)

Toss the Bug

Each child will take a turn tossing "bugs" into the middle of a flower. It is not necessary to mark the distance each participant stands from the flowers. Experience has shown that children need little prompting as to where they should stand. Older children will automatically back up as they feel the need for a challenge. Younger children often stand right next to a flower and simply drop their "bug" in.

To create this activity, you will need the following items:

- four to six 12-inch-diameter plastic baskets for the middles of the flowers (plastic bowls or pots, round boxes, or the equivalent)
- colored paper to reproduce flower petals (six per flower)
- laminate or clear contact paper (enough to cover flower petals)
- large brass brads (one per flower)
- beanbags

(If beanbags are not available, fill yellow and red balloons or colored socks with dried beans or rice. In good budget times, wonderful beanbags in the shape of bugs can be found on the Internet.)

To Make Toss The Bug:

1. Reproduce flower petal patterns on to colored paper—six per flower.
2. Cut out patterns.
3. Laminate or cover patterns with clear contact paper.
4. Punch or drill a 1/4 inch hole through the bottom of the plastic bucket (plastic bowls, or pots, or round boxes).
5. Punch holes at top of each petal (marked by an "X" on pattern).
6. Place six petals together, one on top of the other, and line up hole on underside of basket.
7. Attach all petals to basket using one brad.
8. Spread petals to resemble a flower.
9. Repeat to finish all flowers.
10. Place flowers on the ground approximately four feet apart.

Encourage children to toss the bugs into the middle of the flower. When a child finishes at this station, be sure to praise their efforts and then place a sticker or stamp in the corresponding space on their activity card.

(see Figure 1.42 on page 55)

Teddy Bear Support Materials

Teddy Bear Support Materials run from pages 14 to 55.

Join us for the

Teddy Bear Picnic

Bring your favorite stuffed animal to share in the fun.

Figure 1.1 Publicity Page for "Teddy Bear Picnic"

Figure 1.2 Certificate for "Teddy Bear Picnic"

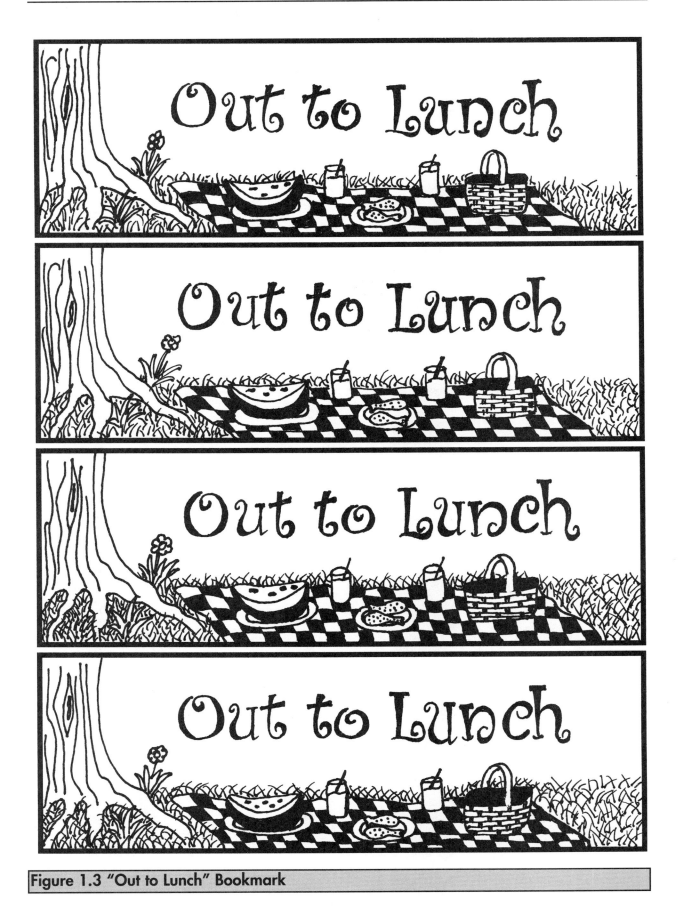

Figure 1.3 "Out to Lunch" Bookmark

Figure 1.4 Activity Card for "Teddy Bear Picnic"

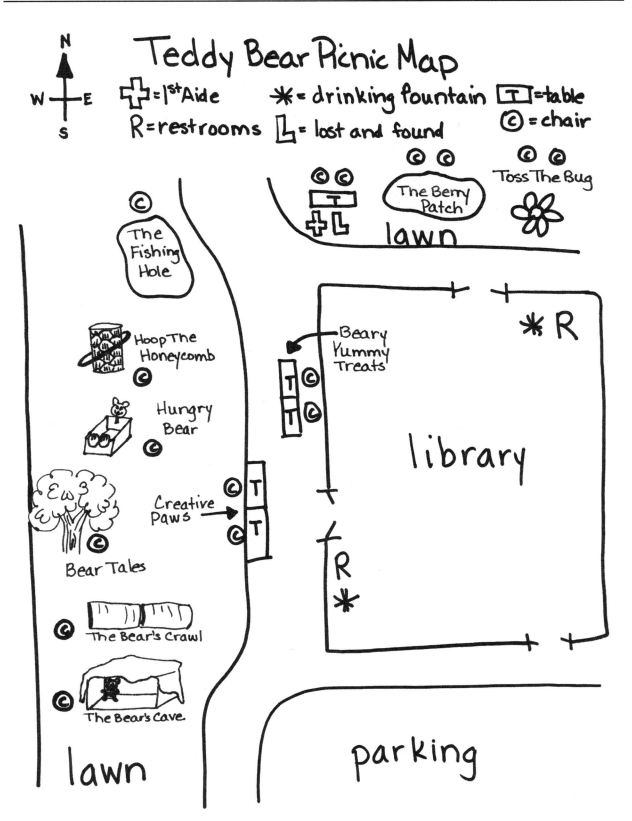

Figure 1.5 Sample Map for "Teddy Bear Picnic"

THE BEAR CRAWL

Figure 1.6 Station Sign for "The Bear Crawl"

Figure 1.7 Station Sign for "Bear Tales"

Figure 1.8 Station Sign for "The Bear's Cave"

Figure 1.9 Station Sign for "Beary Yummy Treats"

Figure 1.10 Station Sign for "The Berry Patch"

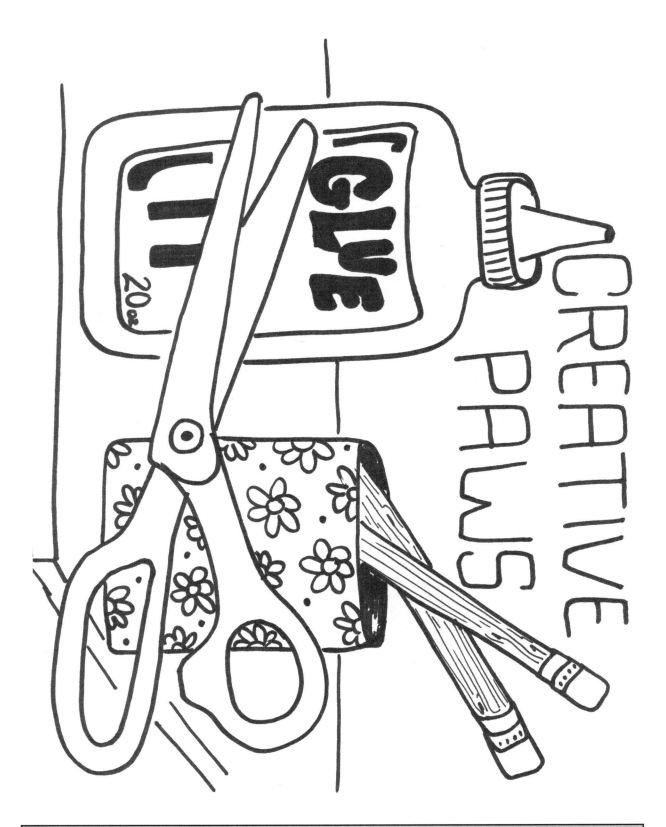

Figure 1.11 Station Sign for "Creative Paws"

Figure 1.12 Station Sign for "The Fishing Hole"

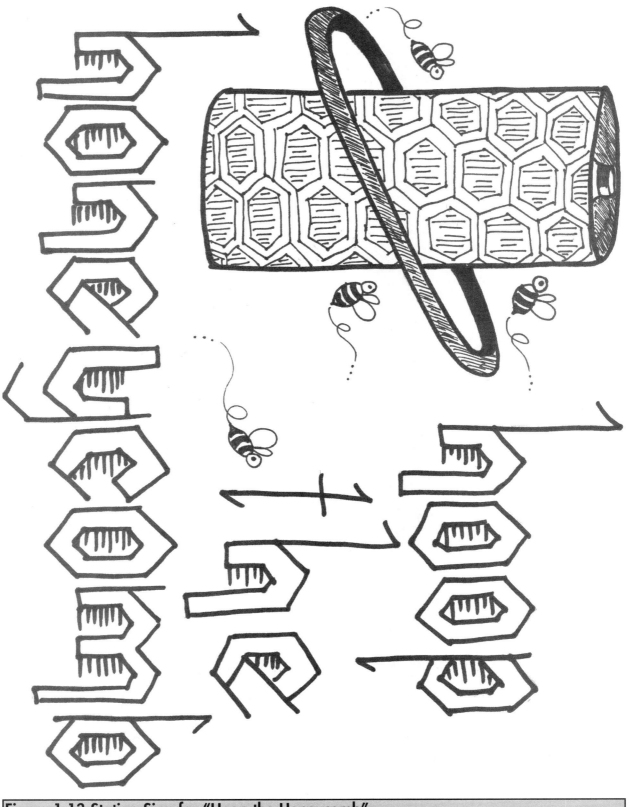

Figure 1.13 Station Sign for "Hoop the Honeycomb"

Figure 1.14 Station Sign for "Hungry Bear"

Figure 1.15 Station Sign for "Toss the Bug"

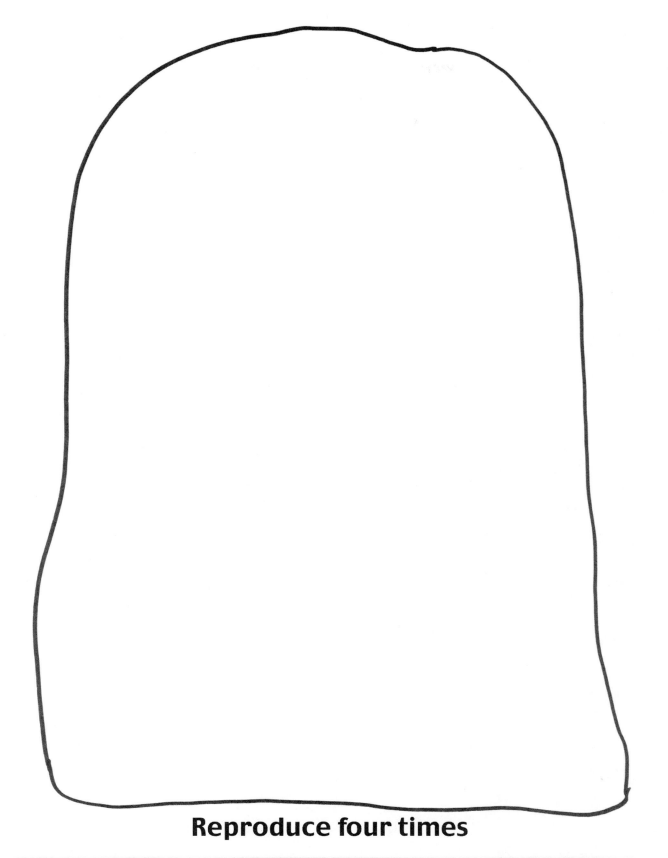

Reproduce four times

Figure 1.16 Rock Pattern for "Bear's Wonderful Day"

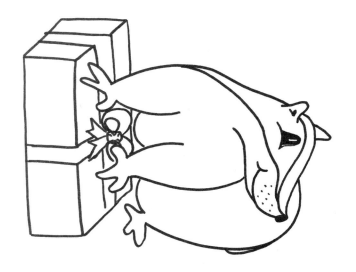

Figure 1.17 Badger Pattern for "Bear's Wonderful Day"

Figure 1.18 Skunk Pattern for "Bear's Wonderful Day"

Figure 1.19 Rabbit Pattern for "Bear's Wonderful Day"

Figure 1.20 Squirrel Pattern for "Bear's Wonderful Day"

Figure 1.21 Bear Pattern for "Bear's Wonderful Day"

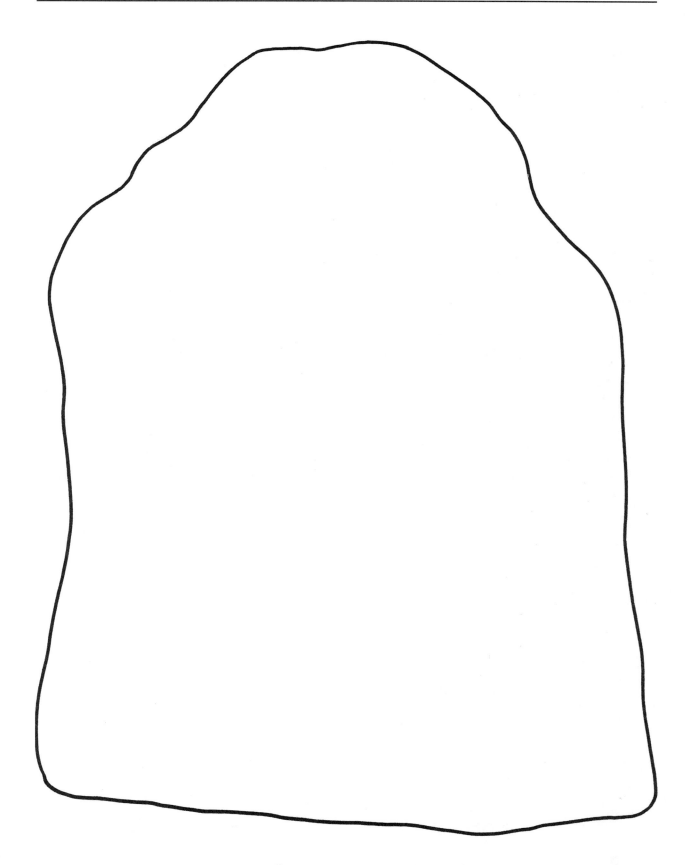

Figure 1.22 Rock to Hide Party Pattern for "Bear's Wonderful Day"

Figure 1.23 Party Rock Pattern for "Bear's Wonderful Day"

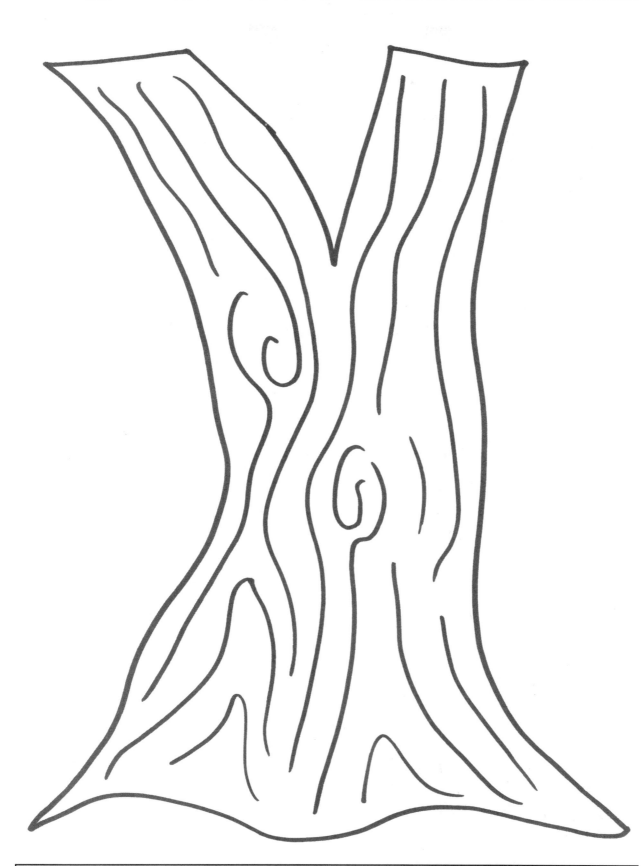

Figure 1.24 Tree Pattern for "Four Little Apples"

Figure 1.25 Tree Pattern for "Four Little Apples"

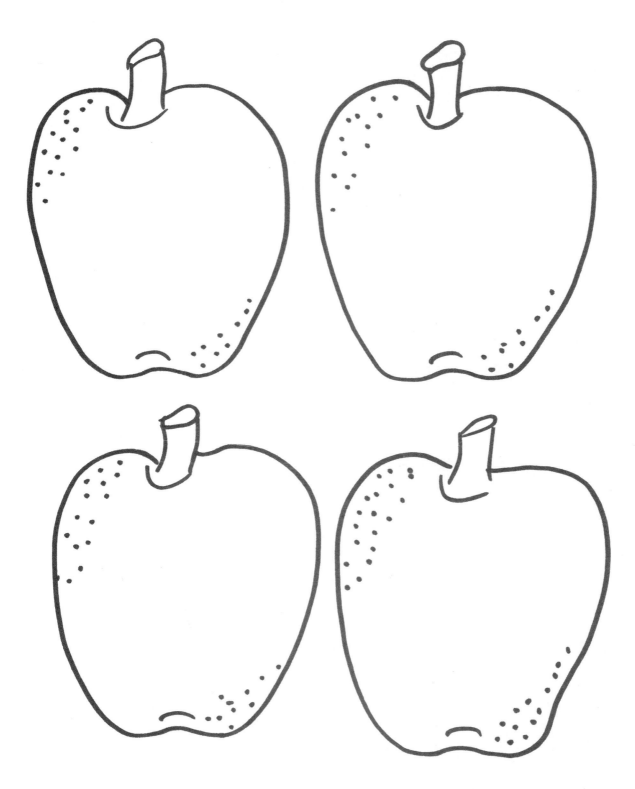

Figure 1.26 Apple Patterns for "Four Little Apples"

1.

2.

3.

4. 5. 6. 7.

8.

Figure 1.27 Illustration of Pom Pom Ant for "Little Ants"

Figure 1.28 Mustache Pattern for "Where is the Picnic?"

Cut one from brown to resemble peanut butter and cut one from purple to resemble jam.

Cut two from white felt for bread.

Figure 1.29 Sandwich Pattern for "Where is the Picnic?"

Figure 1.30 Balloon Bookmark Patterns

To make Beehive Craft:
1. **Cut out all pieces**
2. **Attach one bee behind top of hive marked by dot**
3. **Place brad through hive and bee lining up dots and fasten.**
4. **Attach two bees to each side at dots and fasten.**

Figure 1.31 Bee Patterns for "Beehive Craft"

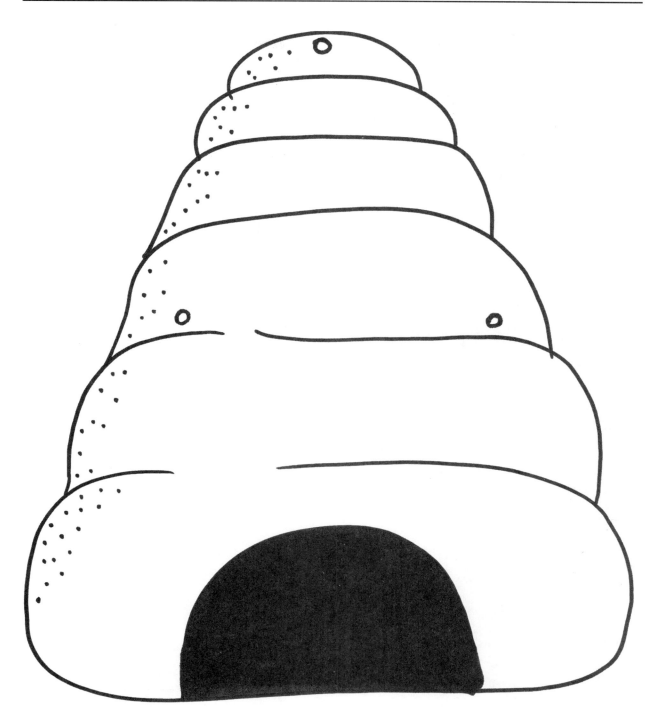

Figure 1.32 Beehive Pattern for "Beehive Craft"

To make Brady Bear:
  1. Cut out all pieces
  2. Attach head, arms, and legs
     at x's using brass brads

Figure 1.33 Pattern for "Brady Bear Craft"

Figure 1.34 Pattern for "Dress the Bear Craft"

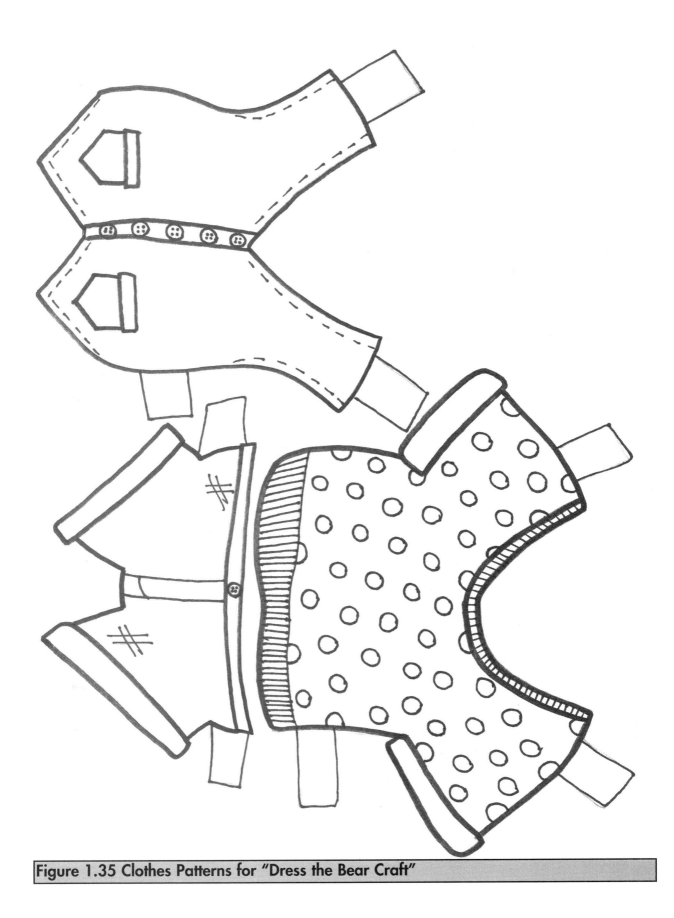

Figure 1.35 Clothes Patterns for "Dress the Bear Craft"

Cut Out

Cut Out

To make the Panda Mask:
1. Cut out.
2. Attach string at dots.

Figure 1.36 Pattern for "Panda Mask Craft"

Figure 1.37 Fish Patterns for "Fishing Hole"

Figure 1.38 Fish Patterns for "Fishing Hole"

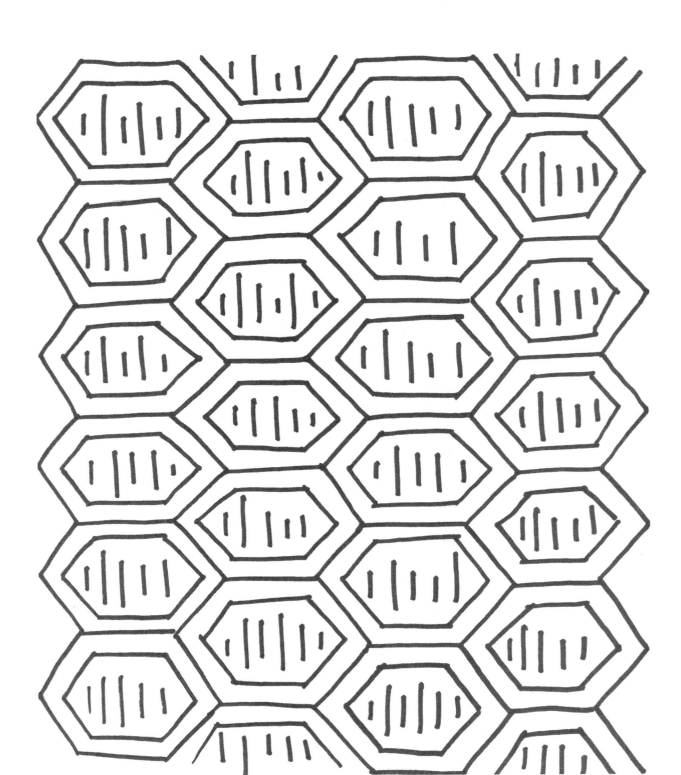

To reproduce this pattern for the craft, enlarge this image 130%.

Figure 1.39 Honeycomb Pattern for "Hoop the Honeycomb"

Figure 1.40 Bear Head Pattern for "Hungry Bear"

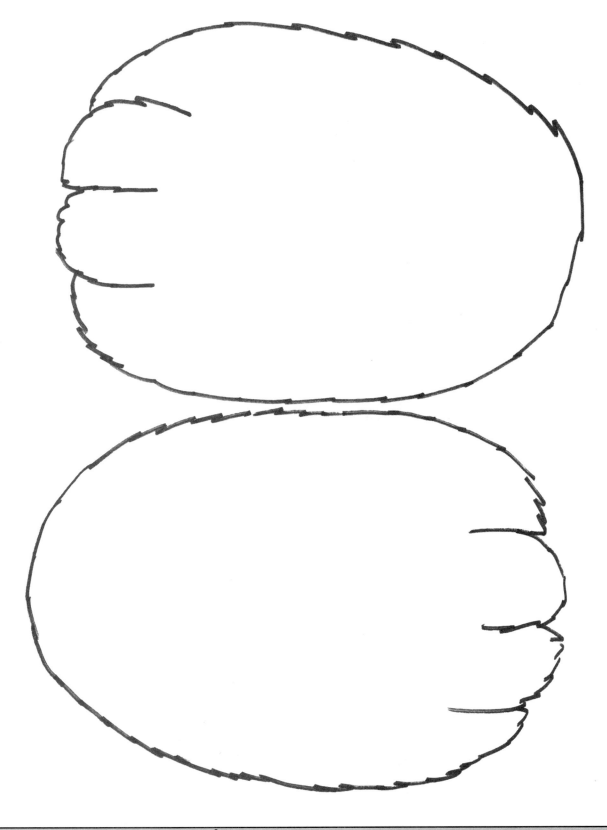

Figure 1.41 Bear Paw Patterns for "Hungry Bear"

Figure 1.42 Flower Petal Pattern for "Toss the Bug"

Winterfest

Description

Winterfest family story and game night is designed to include just that—the entire family! Everything necessary to conduct this wintry delight is provided here, except hot chocolate and a warm cozy room. Winterfest begins by sharing heartwarming interactive stories, moves to fun-filled organized games and activities the entire family will enjoy, and then concludes with a light snack. Provide a snack, (hot chocolate is always a hit on a cold winter's night), or ask parents and caregivers to bring food items to share. Winterfest could even include a chili dinner or potluck. Although this program is geared to the preschool-aged child, you may choose to include an "after hours" game time for families with older children. Furnish games or invite families to bring their favorite board game to share.

Publicity Page

Ready-to-personalize flyers are provided to make advertising your program a snap. To personalize use the CD ROM or simply cut and paste your program information onto the master and then reproduce. Enlarge and color your flyer to create an eye-catching poster for display.

(see Figure 2.1 on page 73)

Certificate

Easy-to-make certificates are wonderful keepsakes for parents and caregivers. Certificates may be handed out at the conclusion of your program (best for small crowds), or simply placed at a table for parents and caregivers to help themselves.

To create certificates, you will need enough paper so that each participant receives one.

To Make Certificates:

1. Use CD ROM and print, type, or cut and paste your library name, logo, date, library director's or mayor's signature, or other information onto certificate pattern.
2. Copy enough certificates—one for each child.

(see Figure 2.2 on page 74)

Bookmarks

Whimsical bookmarks to color may be reproduced and given at any time during your program. You may also choose to distribute them prior to your event, along with the publicity flyer, as a form of advertisement.

(see Figures 2.3, 2.4 on pages 75 to 76)

Station Signs

Station signs identify activities in which children and their parents and caregivers may participate. Winterfest was designed to include eight "game" stations, one "treat" station and one "storytime" station. Assign the storytime station the number one, as all participants will begin at this station and then assign the treat station the number ten, where all participants will end. Divide participants into eight small groups and assign each a beginning station number. Ring "sleigh bells" to signal when it is time for participants to move to another station.

To create station signs, you will need the following items:

- ten pieces of paper or cardstock
- laminate or clear contact paper (enough to cover signs)
- tape

To Make Signs:

1. Reproduce one sign for each station.
2. Color signs.
3. Laminate or cover signs with clear contact paper.
4. Tape station signs on wall or other visible location near each station.

   NOTE: Laminated signs may be used year after year.

   (see Figures 2.5, 2.6, 2.7, 2.8, 2.9, 2.10, 2.11, 2.12, 2.13, 2.14 on pages 77 to 86)

Activities

The following activities are provided for you:

- Carrot Nose for Snowman *(on pages 58 to 59)*
- Freeze Game *(on pages 59 to 60)*
- Ice Fishing *(on pages 60 to 61)*
- Marshmallow Snowman Craft *(on pages 61)*
- Snowball Scoop *(on pages 61 to 62)*
- Snowball Spoon Race *(on pages 62)*
- Snowball Toss *(pages 63)*
- Snowflake Song and Craft *(on pages 63 to 64)*

Carrot Nose for Snowman

Each child will take a turn trying to place a carrot nose on the snowman and then delight in watching older siblings or parents and caregivers try it blindfolded!

To create this game, you will need the following supplies:

- 8 1/2 x 11-inch orange paper (enough to make several carrot noses—pattern provided)
- one large white plastic garbage bag
- one red and one black permanent marker
- scissors
- tape
- blindfold

To Make Snowman:

1. Cut along each side of the plastic bag, stopping at the bottom, and unfold. (This will create a long white plastic sheet.)
2. Draw a snowman using two circles, one for the head and the other, larger circle, for the body.
3. Draw a hat, two eyes, and a mouth (as illustrated)—scarf and buttons optional.

   (see Figure 2.15 on page 87)

To Make Carrot Noses:

1. Reproduce carrot noses onto orange paper.
2. Cut out patterns.
3. Place tape on back of each carrot. (You may choose to write child's name on carrot.)

   (see Figure 2.16 on page 88)

Instructions to Play:

1. Tape the snowman to a wall at a height that children can reach.
2. Give first participant a carrot.
3. Blindfold older participants.
4. Direct the participant to "put the nose on the snowman." (Spinning is optional.)
5. Winner is the participant whose carrot nose is determined to be the closest to actual nose location.

   OPTIONAL: You may choose to omit the blindfold for very young children.

Freeze Game

This simple game has been around for years. Children will move forward when they are shown the "melt" sign and stop, "freezing" in place, when they are shown the "freeze" sign.

To create this game, you will need the following supplies:

- two pieces of white paper or cardstock
- laminate or clear contact paper (enough to cover paper)
- masking tape
- clear tape (book tape works best)

To Make Freeze Game:

1. Reproduce sun pattern *on page 89* onto yellow paper or cardstock.
2. Reproduce ice cube pattern *on page 90* onto blue paper or cardstock.
3. Color signs.
4. Laminate or cover signs with clear contact paper.
5. Place signs back to back and tape all edges.

   (Figures 2.17, 2.18 on pages 89 to 90)

Instructions to Play:

1. Choose one person (or yourself) to be the sign holder.
2. Have participants stand side by side behind masking tape line.
3. Instruct participants to move forward only when the sun "melt" sign is displayed.
4. Instruct participants to stop and freeze in place when the ice cube "freeze" sign is displayed.
5. Any participant who is caught moving after the ice cube sign is displayed must return to masking tape line, and continue to play from there.
6. Winner is the first participant to reach the sign holder.

Ice Fishing

Ice Fishing puts a new spin on the ever-popular fishing activities. Fish are caught through a "hole in the ice," making this fishing game a little more challenging than The Fishing Hole in Chapter One. A paper clip is attached to each fish's mouth and poles are equipped with magnets at the end of cotton string.

To create this game (for twenty participants at a time), you will need the following items:

- twenty wooden dowels in 18-inch lengths (one for each fishing pole)
- cotton string (24 inches per pole)
- roll of self-adhesive magnetic strip (1/2 inch per pole)
- ten empty boxes with lids (typing paper boxes work great)
- white paper or plastic tablecloths (enough to cover each box)
- scissors
- tape
- variety of colored paper to reproduce approximately one hundred fish from patterns
- small paper clips (one per fish)

To Make Ice Fishing:

1. Cut a hole in lid of box large enough for a child to easily remove fish.
2. Cover each box with white paper or plastic tablecloth.

To Make Fish:

1. Reproduce fish from patterns *on pages 91 to 92* using colored paper. (Use both fish patterns to reproduce fish back to back on same piece of paper, creating a front and back to each fish.)

2. Place paperclip on the mouth of each fish.

   (see Figures 2.19, 2.20 on pages 91 to 92)

   OPTIONAL: Provide enough fish for each child to take one or two home.

To Make Fishing Pole:

1. Drill a hole at one end of each dowel—large enough to thread string through.
2. Thread a 24-inch piece of cotton string through each hole and tie knot.
3. Stick a 1/2-inch piece of self adhesive magnet to loose end of each string. (Be sure to cover entire sticky side of magnet with string.)
4. To avoid tangles, when not in use, wrap string around each pole.

Place fish in boxes and let children have fun "catching" and then releasing several fish. Restock as needed.

Marshmallow Snowman Craft

An edible Marshmallow Snowman satisfies not only the sweet and salty tooth, but also the creativity in every child.

To create this craft, you will need the following supplies for each participant:

- one small resealable plastic bag
- three marshmallows (snowman's body)
- two straight pretzels (snowman's arms)
- four red-hot candies (snowman's two eyes and buttons)
- one candy corn (snowman's nose)
- one candy kiss (snowman's hat)

To Make Marshmallow Snowman Craft:

1. Place all supplies on a covered table.
2. Display a completed snowman.
3. Instruct participants to place snowman parts into a plastic bag to take home, or let them assemble at the table, and then place into plastic bag to take home.
4. Marshmallows and candy are stuck on with a small amount of saliva (lick your own!), or provide small dishes of water to "dip" marshmallows into.

   NOTE: If participants will be making their snowmen and eating them immediately, plastic bags will not be necessary.

   (see Figure 2.21 on page 93)

Snowball Scoop

To create this game, you will need to gather the following supplies:

- one bag of white cotton balls
- colorful plastic bucket and shovel (or large metal spoon)
- large plastic or metal bowl

- blindfold
- table
- chair

Instructions to Play:

1. Place the bowl on a table.
2. Scatter the cotton balls on the table next to the bowl.
3. Instruct participant to sit in chair facing the bowl and cotton balls.
4. Blindfold participant and hand them spoon.
5. Instruct participant to scoop as many cotton balls into the bowl as they can when you say "go."
6. Allow each participant one minute.
7. Participants are not allowed to touch the cotton balls but may hold onto the edge of the bowl.
8. Winner is the participant that scoops the most cotton balls into the bowl in allotted time.

   OPTIONAL: You may choose to omit the blindfold for very young children.

Snowball Spoon Race

Remember the old-fashioned potato on a spoon race? Then the Snowball Spoon Race will bring back memories for parents and caregivers and delight those who are experiencing it for the first time.

To create this game, you will need the following supplies:

- six Styrofoam balls or white pompoms (3 inches—purchase or make your own with white yarn)
- masking tape
- six spoons

Instructions to Play:

1. Mark beginning and end of race with a long piece of masking tape.
2. Instruct participants to stand side by side, behind masking tape line.
3. Give each participant a spoon with a ball or pompom on it.
4. Instruct participants to hold spoon with one hand and place the other behind their backs.
5. Instruct participants to walk to the other end of the room without dropping their ball or pompom when you say, "GO!"
6. If a participant drops ball or pompom have them stop, pick it up and continue the race.
7. Winner is the first to cross masking tape at opposite side of room.

   OPTIONAL: If children are competing with adults, instruct adults to start from beginning if they drop their ball or pompom.

Snowball Toss

Tossing snowballs is fun at any age! Parents and caregivers will certainly appreciate the warm, dry variety used in this game. Snowballs are tossed through the center of a snowman and not at each other!

To create this game, you will need the following supplies:

- one large white foam board
- six long brass brads
- razor or hobby knife
- several Styrofoam balls or white recycled paper crumpled into a ball (3 inches)

To Make Snowman:

1. Draw a circle as close to the edge of the foam board as possible. (A pencil with string attached is an excellent tool. Simply tie string to pencil, then place "loose" end of string in the middle of foam board. Hold string taut and draw circle.)
2. Draw another circle 2 inches from the inside of the first one.
3. Draw last circle 2 inches from the inside of the second circle.
4. Cut on all lines creating three rings, each 2 inches wide.
5. Place the rings, largest one at the bottom and smallest at the top, to create a snowman.
6. Slightly overlap edges and secure rings to each other using two brads at each edge.
7. Prop snowman in a corner or suspend from the ceiling. Let children toss the snowballs through the rings.

(see Figure 2.22 on page 94)

Snowflake Craft

This "snowflake" will be used with the Snowflake Song. *Play number three from the CD*, follow the lyrics and have fun as your snowflake dances!

To create one snowflake, you will need the following supplies:

- one white Styrofoam plate (6 inches)
- three white and two blue crepe paper strips (each 12 inches)
- stapler and staples

To Make Snowflake:

1. Staple the crepe paper strips (starting with white and alternating colors) side by side to the edge of Styrofoam plate.
2. Create one snowflake for each participant by multiplying all supplies.
3. Now you are ready to sing "Snowflake Song."

Snowflake Song

(Distribute one snowflake per participant and encourage children and their parents and caregivers to follow you snowflake's dance. Play number three from CD.)

NOTE: "Snowflake Song" is the most fun when all participants stand in a circle, facing in.

See the snowflakes on my hair, on my knee, and in the air;
  (Place snowflake on hair, move to knee, and then wave in the air.)
Now they're falling on my nose, on my tummy, on my toes.
  (Place snowflake on nose, move to tummy, and then to toes.)
Whirling, twirling all around, snowflakes falling on the ground;
  (Drop snowflake.)
Snowflakes falling everywhere, swirling snowflakes in the air.
  (Pick up snowflake and wave in the air.)
See the snowflakes on my hip, on my arm, and on my lip;
  (Place snowflake on hip, move to arm, and then lip.)
Now they're falling at my side, on my back they try to hide.
  (Wave snowflake at side and then hide behind back.)
Whirling, twirling all around, snowflakes falling on the ground;
  (Drop snowflake.)
Snowflakes falling everywhere, swirling snowflakes in the air.
  (Pick up snowflake and wave in the air.)
See the snowflakes on my hair, on my knee, and in the air;
  (Place snowflake on hair, move to knee, and then wave in the air.)
Now they're falling on my nose, on my tummy, on my toes.
  (Place snowflake on nose, move to tummy, and then to toes.)
Whirling, twirling all around, snowflakes falling on the ground;
  (Drop snowflake.)
Snowflakes falling everywhere, swirling snowflakes in the air.
  (Pick up snowflake and wave in the air.)
See the snowflakes on my hip, on my arm, and on my lip;
  (Place snowflake on hip, move to arm, and then lip.)
Now they're falling at my side, on my back they try to hide.
  (Wave snowflake at side and then hide behind back.)
Whirling, twirling all around, snowflakes falling on the ground;
  (Drop snowflake.)
Snowflakes falling everywhere, swirling snowflakes in the air.
  (Pick up snowflake and wave in the air.)

OPTIONAL: You may want to reproduce the words on a large piece of paper, for all to see.

Stories

The following stories and patterns are provided for you:
- Build a Snowman *(on pages 65 to 66)*
- Hungry Farm Animals *(on pages 66 to 67)*
- In the House *(on pages 67 to 69)*
- Little White Mice *(on pages 69 to 70)*
- Wake Up Bear *(on pages 70 to 72)*

Build a Snowman

(Play number four from CD.)
Roll the snowballs now with me.
(Roll hands around each other.)
Build a snowman one, two, three.
(Count to three with fingers.)
Place the snowballs in a row.
(Place largest snowball at bottom of flannel board, then medium-sized above first snowball, and smallest at top.)
Small on top and big below.
(Point to small snowball and then largest snowball.)
Sticks for arms
(Place arms on snowman.)
and a carrot nose.
(Place nose where a snowman's nose would be located.)
Button eyes
(Place eyes.)
and a smile that glows.
(Place mouth on snowman.)
Place a tall hat on his head.
(Place hat at top of head.)
A pair of mittens
(Place mittens over stick hands.)
and a scarf of red.
(Place scarf at neck.)
Now it's time to take a rest
(Rest cheek on praying hands.)
and drink hot chocolate it's the best!
(Pretend to drink and then give thumbs up.)
Very tasty down it goes,
(Move hands from neck to toes.)
warming up my toes.
(Point at toes.)
Making snowmen is such fun,
(Pretend to pack snowballs.)
now let's build another one.
(Continue packing snow.)
Gather up a lot more snow,
(Pretend to scoop up snow.)
ready, set, let's go!
(Raise arms in air and yell.)

> NOTE: CD repeats song three times. Follow flannel board directions the first time through; then see if you can keep up as the song goes faster, using actions to match the words.

To Make as a Flannel Story:

1. Cut all patterns from felt as indicated on patterns.
2. Enhance with felt markers.

    (see Figures 2.23, 2.24, 2.25, 2.26, 2.27, 2.28 on pages 95 to 100)

To Make as a Magnetic story:

1. Reproduce patterns.
2. Color all patterns in colors of your choice.
3. Laminate patterns.
4. Cut out patterns.
5. Attach a magnetic strip to the back of each piece.

    (see Figures 2.23, 2.24, 2.25, 2.26, 2.27, 2.28 on pages 95 to 100)

    OPTIONAL: Use Completed Build a Snowman illustration as a coloring sheet.

    (see Figure 2.29 on page 101)

Hungry Farm Animals

(Before you begin, place farm flannel board opened on easel or in front of a traditional flannel board.)
Here is the hungry duck all soft and downy,
(Place duck on flannel board middle section.)
Who quacks from her nest in the hay, "Quack, quack."
(Encourage children to make quacking sound.)
Here is the hungry pig fat and muddy,
(Place pig on board's middle section.)
Who oinks beside his tray, "Oink, oink."
(Encourage children to make oinking sound.)
Here is the hungry cow black and white,
(Place cow on board's middle section.)
Who moos as she nods her head, "Moooooo."
(Encourage children to make mooing sound.)
Here is the farmer who feeds them at night,
(Place farmer on board's middle section.)
In the warm barn, then locks the doors tight!
(Fold barn doors closed and latch with hinge.)

> NOTE: Placing animals in the middle section will ensure they don't fall when the doors are closed.

To Make as a Flannel Story:

1. Cut all patterns from felt colors of your choice.
2. Enhance with felt markers.

OR

1. Reproduce patterns.

2. Color all patterns in colors of your choice.

3. Laminate patterns.

4. Cut out patterns.

5. Using double-stick tape, attach felt strips to the back of each piece.

   (see Figures 2.30, 2.31, 2.32, 2.33, 2.34 on pages 102 to 106)

To create the barn flannel board, you will need the following supplies:

- white glue
- scissors
- hole punch
- one large red poster board
- four green felt squares
- four blue felt squares
- two brass brads
- two pieces of 8 1/2 x 11-inch white paper

To Make Barn Flannel Board:

1. Lay poster board horizontally.

2. Measure 4 inches down from the top edge and draw a line across entire width.

3. Cut on dotted line, as shown in Figure "A," and set aside.

4. Find the center of the horizontal poster board.

5. Fold right edge to center and crease firmly.

6. Fold left edge to center and crease firmly.

7. With right corner folded, cut off a triangular piece to create corner of barn's roof, as shown in Figure "B."

8. Use triangular piece as pattern for left corner.

9. Cut white paper into 1-inch strips and other shapes of your choice.

10. Decorate barn by gluing strips and shapes as shown.

11. Cut a 1 x 3-inch piece from poster board strip (left from step three) to create barn door latch.

12. Punch hole in one end of door latch and make a notch (facing down) in the other end.

13. Center door latch over closed barn doors and attach with brad.

14. Attach remaining brad to opposite door. (The notched end will slide behind brad to "lock" door.)

15. Tape brads open on the inside of barn.

16. Glue blue felt squares to top section of inside of barn to make the sky.

17. Cut hill shape on one side of each green felt square.

18. Glue green felt to bottom for grass and blue felt to top for sky.

    (see Figure 2.35 on page 107)

In the House

(This song can be sung to "If You're Happy and You Know It." Before beginning, place the pets on the board in the following order: fish, cat, bird, frog, and dog. Then cover each one with a house.)

Can you guess what kind of pet is in the house?
   (Point to first house.)
Can you guess what kind of pet is in the house?
It would swim around so cute without a bathing suit.
   (Pretend to swim.)
Can you guess what kind of pet is in the house?
   (Point to house and then remove house to reveal the fish.)
Yell—"A FISH!"
Can you guess what kind of pet is in the house?
   (Point to second house.)
Can you guess what kind of pet is in the house?
It would sleep and sleep all day and chase the mice away.
   (Place cheek on praying hands and then run in place.)
Can you guess what kind of pet is in the house?
   (Point to house and then remove house to reveal the cat.)
Yell—"A CAT!"
Can you guess what kind of pet is in the house?
   (Point to third house.)
Can you guess what kind of pet is in the house?
It would sing so very sweet and like seeds for a treat.
   (Point to mouth and then pretend to eat.)
Can you guess what kind of pet is in the house?
   (Point to house and then remove house to reveal the bird.)
Yell—"A BIRD!"
Can you guess what kind of pet is in the house?
   (Point to fourth house.)
Can you guess what kind of pet is in the house?
It would hop and hop around and eat bugs off the ground.
   (Hop in place and then pretend to eat.)
Can you guess what kind of pet is in the house?
   (Point to house and then remove house to reveal the frog.)
Yell—"A FROG!"
Can you guess what kind of pet is in the house?
   (Point to fifth house.)
Can you guess what kind of pet is in the house?
It would bark to guard the place and slobber on your face.
   (Bark and then make licking motion with tongue.)
Can you guess what kind of pet is in the house?
   (Point to house and then remove house to reveal the dog.)
Yell—"A DOG!"

To Make as a Flannel Story:

1. Cut five houses from felt colors of your choice.
2. Cut all other patterns from felt colors of your choice.
3. Enhance with felt markers.

To Make as a Magnetic Story:

1. Reproduce patterns.
2. Color all patterns in colors of your choice.
3. Laminate patterns.
4. Cut out patterns.
5. Attach a magnetic strip to the back of each piece.

   (see Figures 2.36, 2.37, 2.38, 2.39, 2.40, 2.41 on pages 108 to 113)

   OPTIONAL: Copy house onto heavy card stock, laminate, and then glue or tape to the front of a cardboard box. Place stuffed animals inside the box and then pull out each pet as you yell their name.

Little White Mice

(Before you begin, place sun on flannel board.)
Little white mice love to run and to play,
   (Place mice on flannel board.)
When it's dark outside and the sun's gone away.
   (Remove sun from flannel board.)
They scamper through straw all golden and new,
   (Place straw under mice.)
Looking for seeds to hoard and to chew.
   (Place seeds to right of mice.)
They tear up some paper and make a nice nest,
   (Place paper nest under mice and on top of straw.)
As the sun starts to come up, they take a short rest.
   (Place sun on flannel board.)
I love my pet mice and they love me too.
   (Place hands over heart.)
'Cause I provide them a home with a wonderful view!
   (Place aquarium over all flannel pieces.)
NOTE: Prior to telling the story, practice placement of pieces, to ensure all pieces will fit within the aquarium.

To Make as a Flannel Story:

1. Cut mice from white felt and other patterns in colors of your choice.
2. Enhance with felt markers.

To Make as a Magnetic Story:

1. Reproduce patterns.
2. Leave mice white and color all other patterns in colors of your choice.
3. Laminate patterns.
4. Cut out patterns.
5. Attach a magnetic strip to the back of each piece.

   (see Figures 2.42, 2.43 on pages 114 to 115)

To create an aquarium you will need the following supplies:

- one piece of used laminating film, approximately 8 x 11 inches (or two pieces of clear contact paper—sticky sides together)
- enough felt (or paper if making a magnetic story) to create a 1-inch aquarium border doubled (i.e., if outside edge of aquarium measures 8 x 11 inches, you will need 8 inches plus 8 inches plus 11 inches plus 11 inches times 2 = 76 inches)
- double stick tape

To Make Aquarium:

1. Cut felt (or paper) into one-inch strips.
2. Using double stick tape, attach felt (or paper) to outside edges of laminate or clear contact paper.
3. Repeat step two for reverse side of aquarium.
4. Refer to illustration on page 115 for picture (Figure 2.43).

Wake Up Bear

(Before you begin, place rocks, leaves, and dirt from left to right and centered at bottom of board. Place river at left middle.)

One by one, the animals of the forest woke up from their long winter sleep.

(Place sun at middle top of flannel board.)

White Rabbit stretched and yawned—hopping out into the sunshine looking among the rocks for green grass to eat.

(Place rabbit on board near rocks.)

Brown Mouse stretched and yawned—scurrying out into the sunshine searching under the leaves for seeds to eat.

(Place mouse on board near leaves.)

Grey Squirrel stretched and yawned—climbing out into the sunshine digging in the dirt for nuts to eat.

(Place squirrel on board near dirt.)

Striped Raccoon stretched and yawned—creeping out into the sunshine watching along the river for fish to eat.

(Place raccoon on board near river, and then move each animal to the river with raccoon, as you say:)

One by one, all the animals met Striped Raccoon at the river for a drink of water.

They greeted each other and talked about spring and the warm sunshine.

Striped Raccoon laughed and said, "Here we all are, but where is Black Bear?"

White Rabbit answered, "You know Black Bear, he's always the last one to wake up!"

"Yes," said Brown Mouse. "He sure likes to sleep."

"We won't see him for a while yet," said Brown Squirrel.

Striped Raccoon smiled, "I think we should wake him up."

One by one, all the animals agreed to wake up Black Bear. "Yes!" "Let's do it!" "Good idea!" they all shouted together.

Black Bear lived on the side of a hill.

(Place sleeping bear at middle right on board.)

The animals could hear Black Bear snoring.

(Snore loudly.)

Brown Mouse said, "I don't know if he's going to like this."

(Place mouse near bear.)

Brown Squirrel said, "I don't know if WE'RE going to like it either!"

(Place squirrel near bear.)

But Striped Raccoon didn't say anything; he just smiled and crept closer.

(Place raccoon near bear's head.)

One by one, all the animals stood around Black Bear, who was fast asleep.

Brown Mouse laid the seeds he had brought right under Black Bear's nose.

(Place seeds under bear's nose.)

"The smell of seeds should wake him up!" said Brown Mouse.

But Black Bear slept on.

(Snore loudly.)

White Rabbit tickled Black Bear's nose with the green spring grass he had brought.

(Lay grass on bear's nose.)

"This tickly grass should wake him up," he said.

But Black Bear slept on.

(Snore loudly.)

Striped Raccoon, who had not said a word since leaving the river, stepped closer. He leaned over Black Bear's face.

(Move raccoon closer.)

Striped Raccoon sprayed him with the water he had carried in his mouth.

(Make "raspberry" sound.)

Black Bear snorted and growled. He lumbered and howled.

(Snort and growl.)

Striped Raccoon, Grey Squirrel, White Rabbit, and Brown Mouse ran away as fast as they could.

(Remove each animal and place them in your hand as you name them, then place each animal under the river as you say:)

One by one, all the forest animals met at the river where they giggled and laughed. *(Giggle and laugh.)*

(Remove "sleeping" bear and place "laughing" bear above the river as you say:)

Even Black Bear, who laughed the loudest.

(Laugh in deep bear voice.)

To Make as a Magnetic Story:

1. Reproduce patterns.
2. Color all patterns in colors of your choice.
3. Laminate patterns.
4. Cut out patterns.
5. Attach a magnetic strip to the back of each piece.

    (see Figures 2.44, 2.45, 2.46, 2.47, 2.48, 2.49 on pages 116 to 121)

Crispy Snowball Treat

A new twist to a favorite crispy treat made from rice cereal and marshmallows.
To create Crispy Snowball, you will need:

- all of the ingredients to follow your favorite crispy rice cereal treat recipe
- small plastic resealable plastic bags (one for each participant)
- powdered sugar

1. Make crispy rice cereal treat, but do not press into a greased pan; instead, roll into small balls.
2. Place a small amount of powdered sugar (approximately 1-2 teaspoons) into a resealable plastic bag.
3. Let children shake a crispy rice ball in the powdered sugar bag to give it a dusting of "snow."

    OPTIONAL: If resources are available, you may decide to make snow cones or homemade ice cream.

Winterfest Support Materials

Winterfest Support Materials run from pages 73 to 121.

Figure 2.1 Publicity Page for "Winterfest"

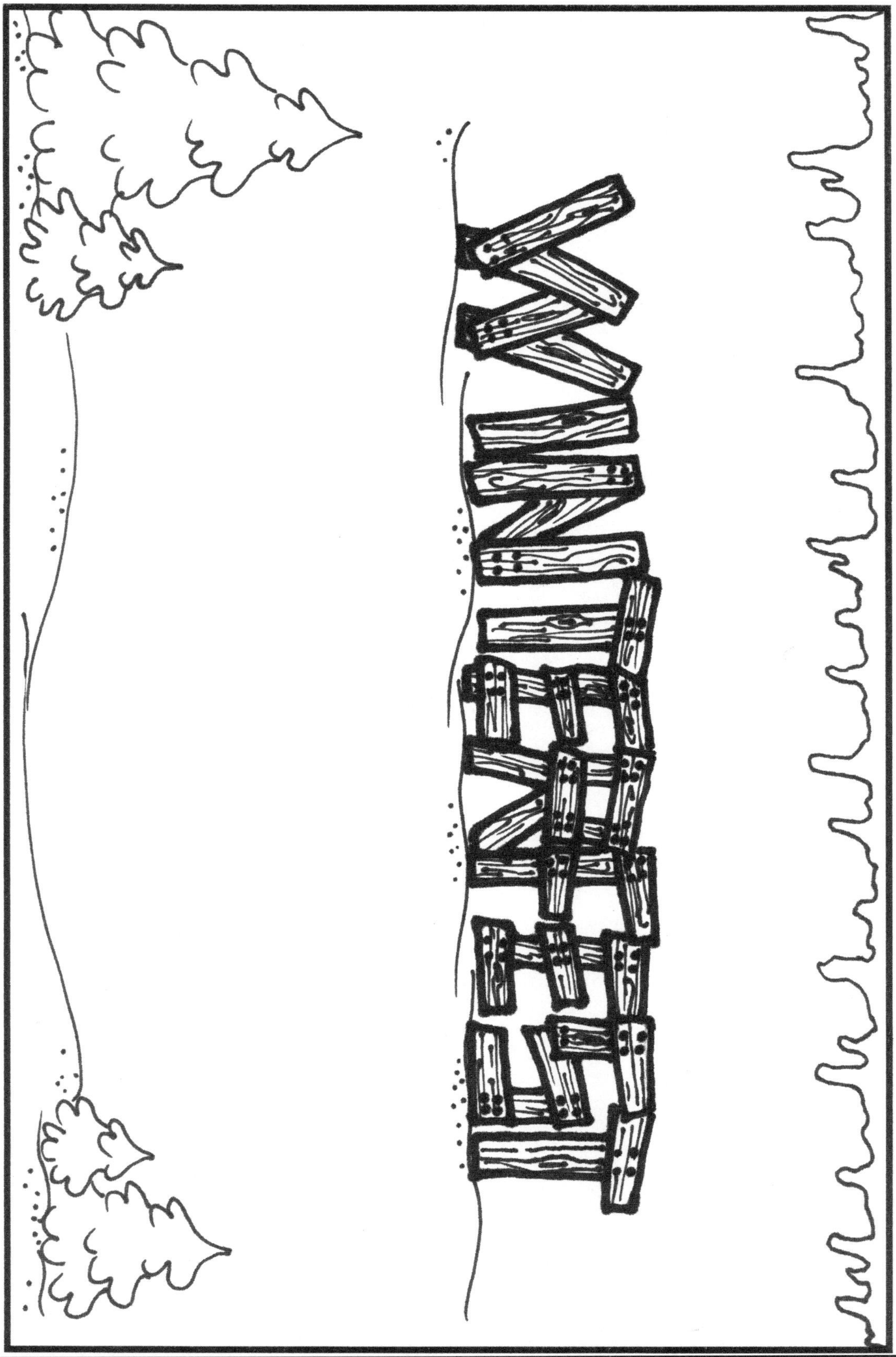

Figure 2.2 Certificate for "Winterfest"

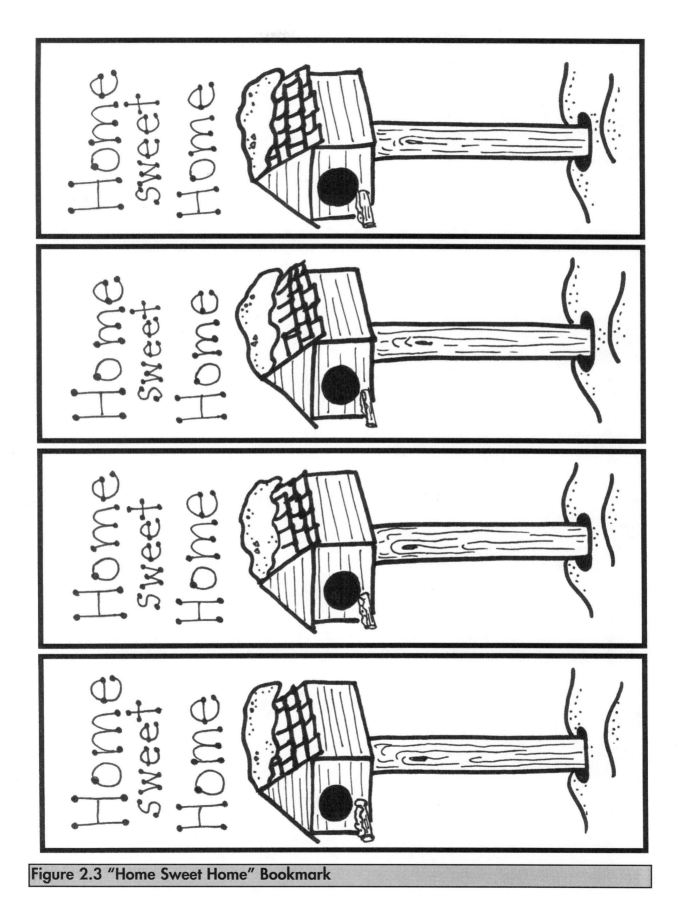

Figure 2.3 "Home Sweet Home" Bookmark

Figure 2.4 "I Love Books" Bookmark

Figure 2.5 Station Sign for "Winterfest"

Figure 2.6 Station Sign for "Winterfest"

Figure 2.7 Station Sign for "Winterfest"

Figure 2.8 Station Sign for "Winterfest"

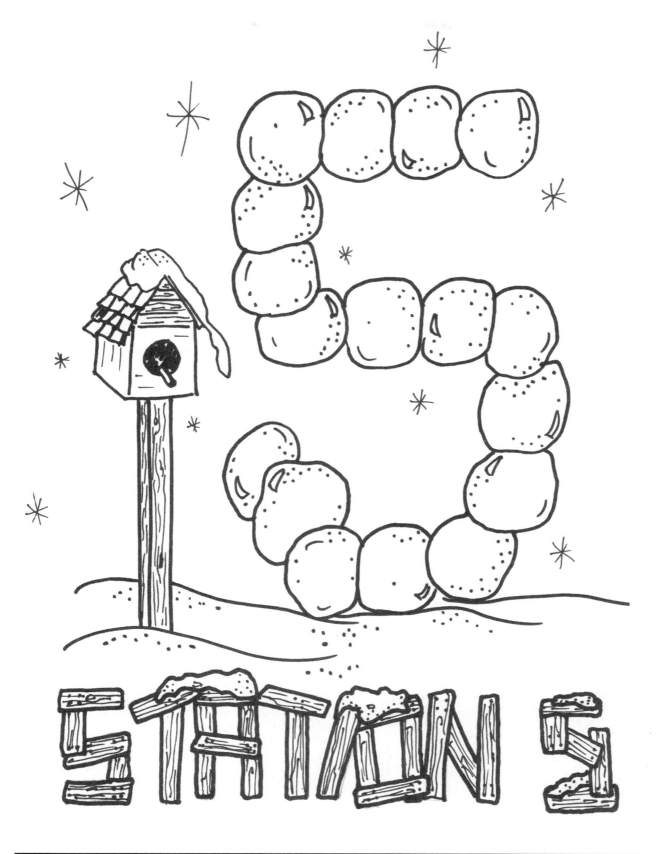

Figure 2.9 Station Sign for "Winterfest"

Figure 2.10 Station Sign for "Winterfest"

Figure 2.11 Station Sign for "Winterfest"

Figure 2.12 Station Sign for "Winterfest"

Figure 2.13 Station Sign for "Winterfest"

Figure 2.14 Station Sign for "Winterfest"

Figure 2.15 Snowman Pattern for "Carrot Nose For Snowman"

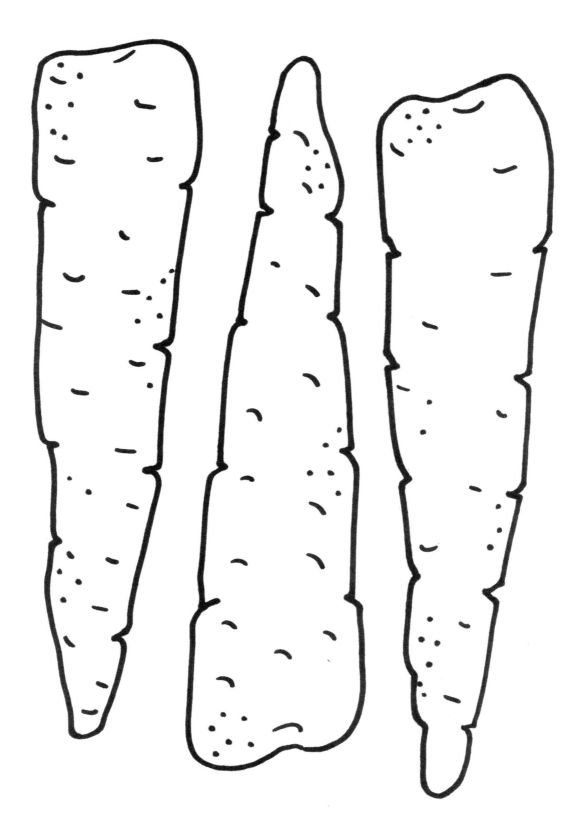

Figure 2.16 Nose Pattern for "Carrot Nose For Snowman"

Figure 2.17 Melt Sign for "Freeze Game"

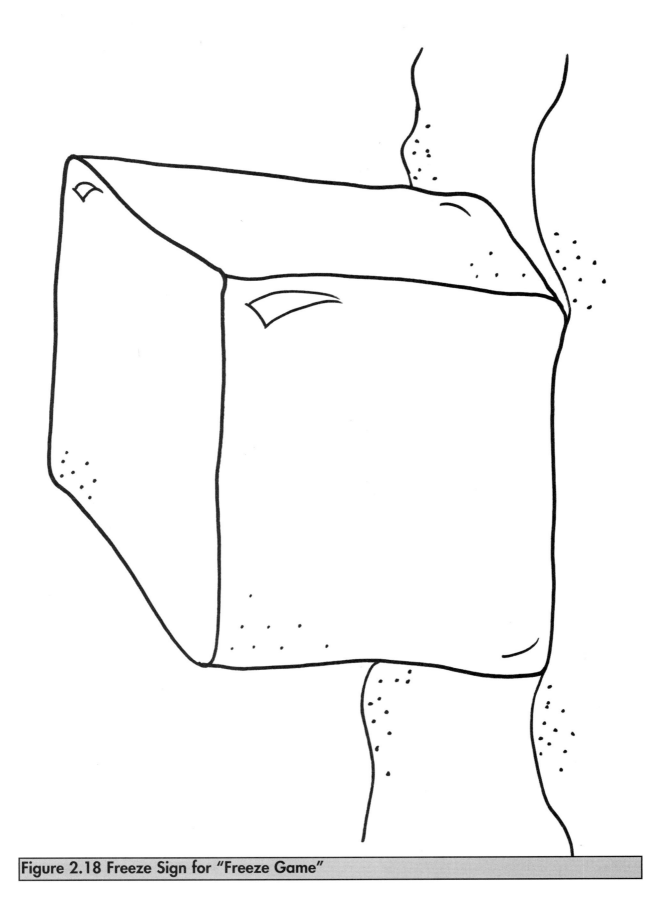

Figure 2.18 Freeze Sign for "Freeze Game"

Figure 2.19 Fish Patterns for "Ice Fishing"

Figure 2.20 Fish Patterns for "Ice Fishing"

Figure 2.21 Illustration for "Marshmallow Snowman Craft"

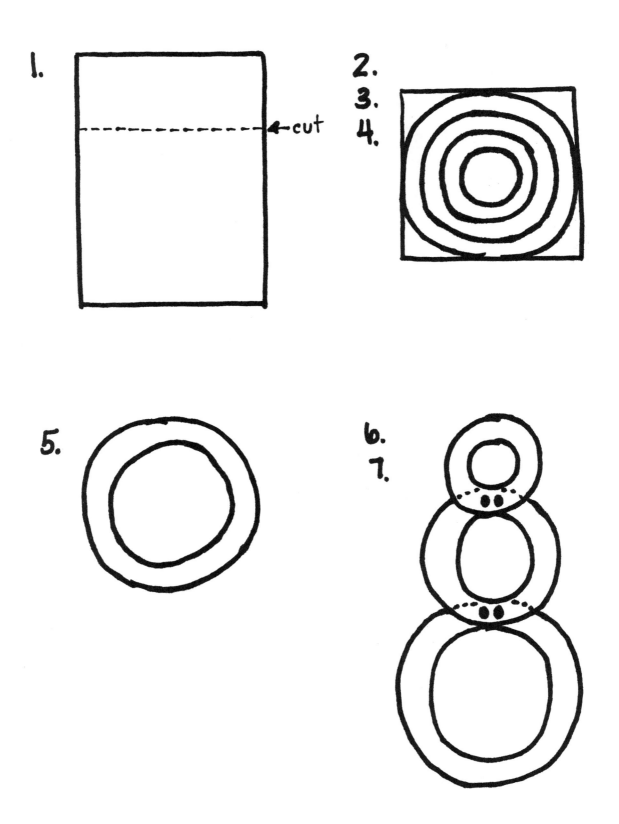

Figure 2.22 Illustration for "Snowball Toss"

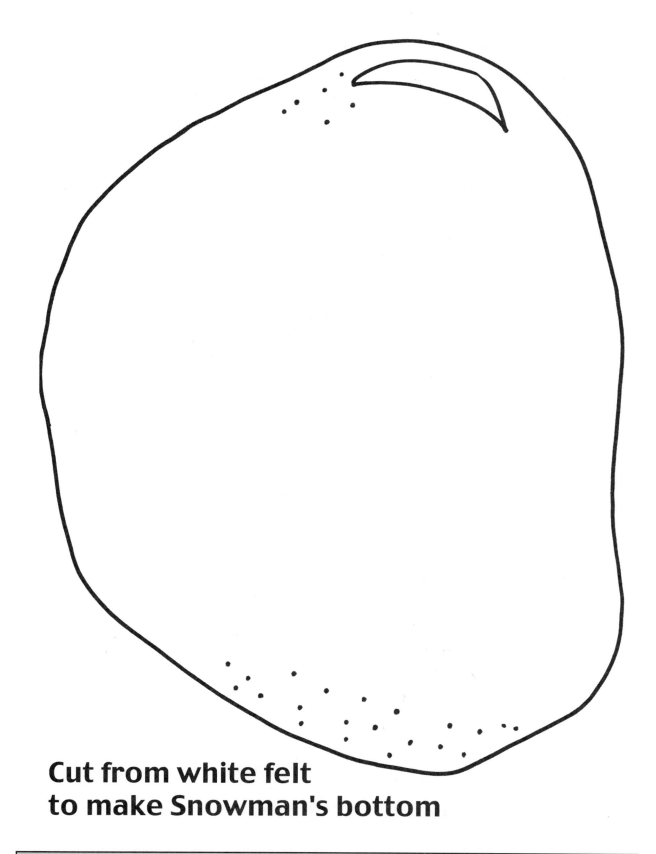

**Cut from white felt
to make Snowman's bottom**

Figure 2.23 Snowball Pattern for "Build a Snowman"

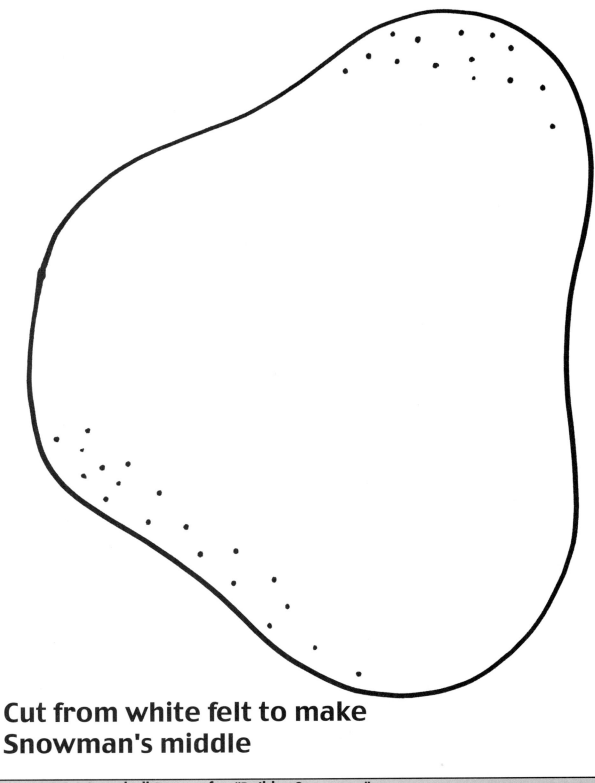

Cut from white felt to make Snowman's middle

Figure 2.24 Snowball Pattern for "Build a Snowman"

Cut from orange felt to make Snowman's nose

Cut from blue felt to make Snowman's eyes

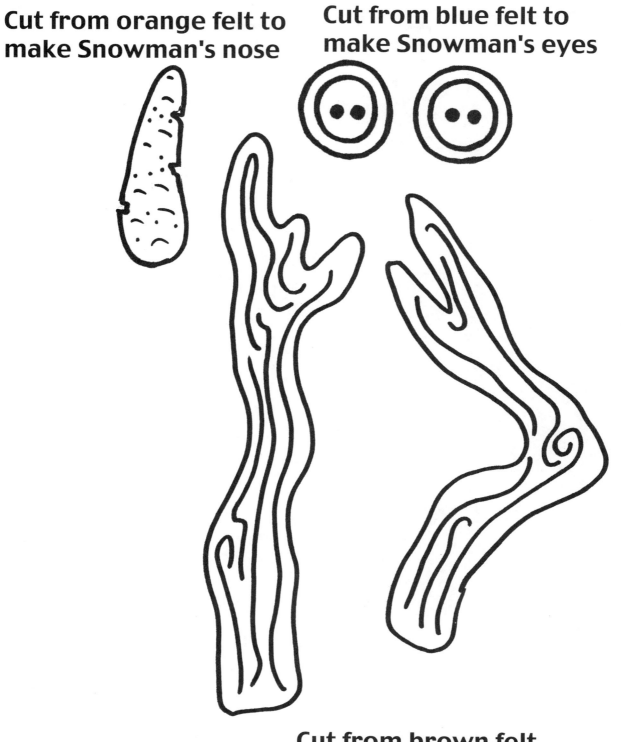

Cut from brown felt to make Snowman's arms

Figure 2.25 Snowman's Nose, Eyes, and Arms Patterns for "Build a Snowman"

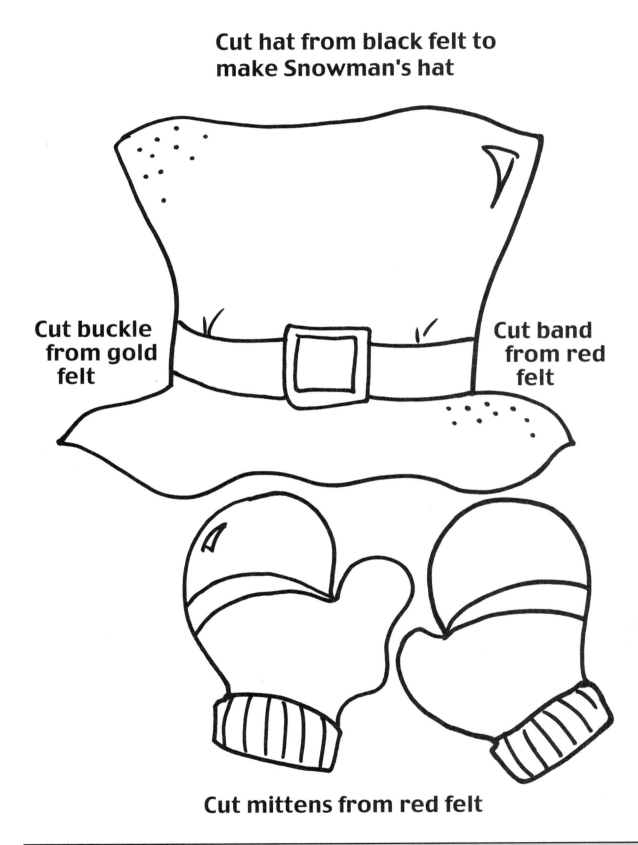

Cut hat from black felt to make Snowman's hat

Cut buckle from gold felt

Cut band from red felt

Cut mittens from red felt

Figure 2.26 Snowman's Hat and Mitten Patterns for "Build a Snowman"

Cut from red felt to make Snowman's scarf

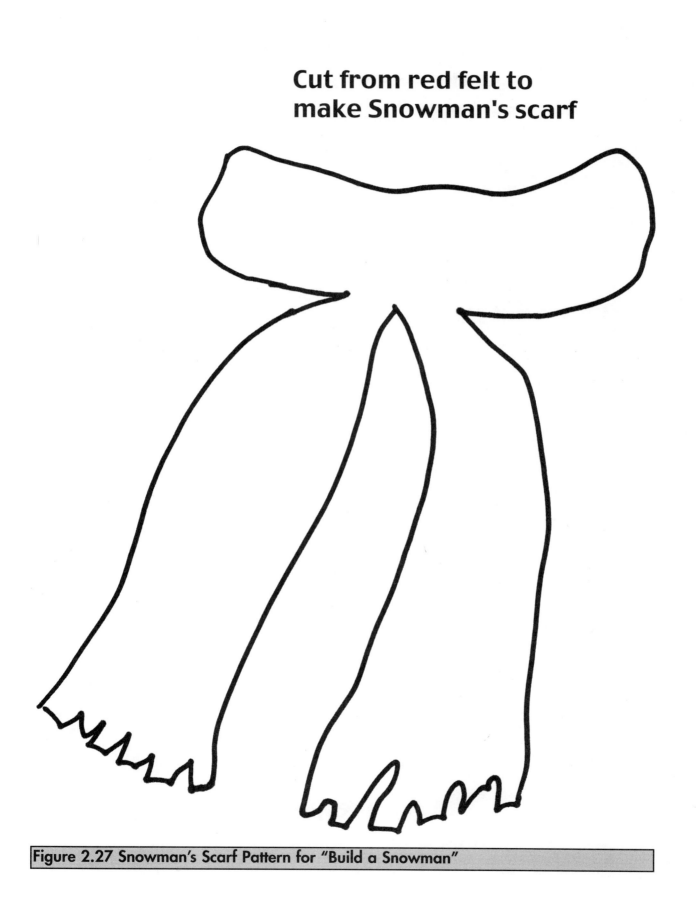

Figure 2.27 Snowman's Scarf Pattern for "Build a Snowman"

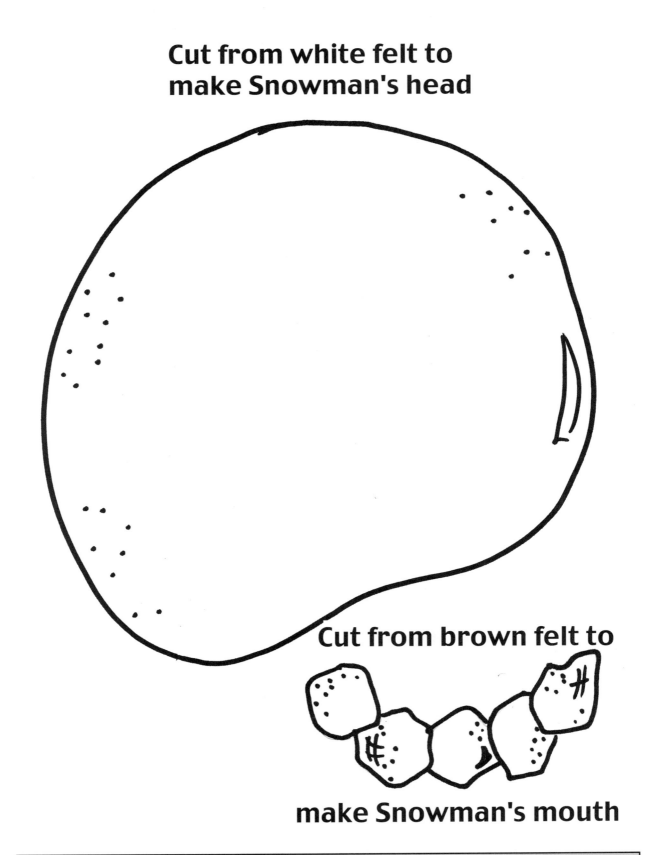

Cut from white felt to make Snowman's head

Cut from brown felt to make Snowman's mouth

Figure 2.28 Snowball and Mouth Patterns for "Build a Snowman"

Figure 2.29 Illustration for Completed "Build a Snowman"

Figure 2.30 Duck Pattern for "Hungry Farm Animals"

Figure 2.31 Pig Pattern for "Hungry Farm Animals"

Figure 2.32 Cow Pattern for "Hungry Farm Animals"

Figure 2.33 Dog Pattern for "Hungry Farm Animals"

Figure 2.34 Farmer Pattern for "Hungry Farm Animals"

Figure A

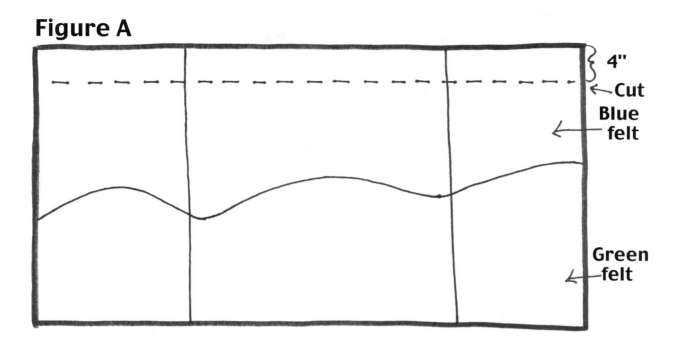

4"
←Cut
Blue felt

Green felt

Figure B

White paper squares

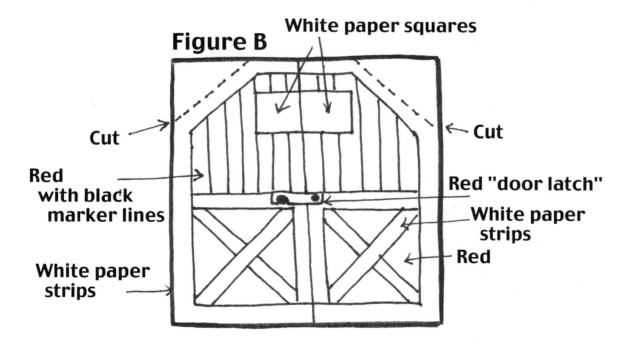

Cut

Cut

Red with black marker lines

Red "door latch"

White paper strips

Red

White paper strips

Figure 2.35 Flannel Board Barn Backdrop Illustration for "Hungry Farm Animals"

Cut out five houses

Figure 2.36 House Pattern for "In the House"

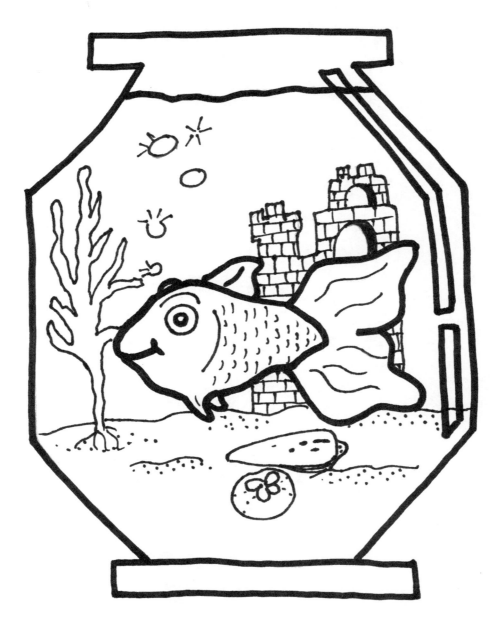

Figure 2.37 Fish Pattern for "In the House"

Figure 2.38 Cat Pattern for "In the House"

Figure 2.39 Bird Pattern for "In the House"

Figure 2.40 Frog Pattern for "In the House"

Figure 2.41 Dog Pattern for "In the House"

Figure 2.42 Sun and Mice Patterns for "Little White Mice"

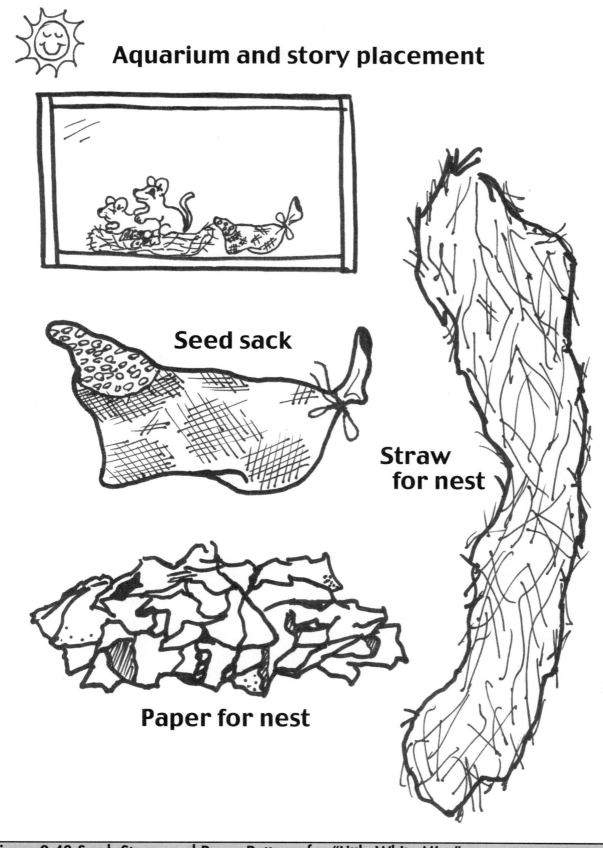

Aquarium and story placement

Seed sack

Straw for nest

Paper for nest

Figure 2.43 Seed, Straw, and Paper Patterns for "Little White Mice"

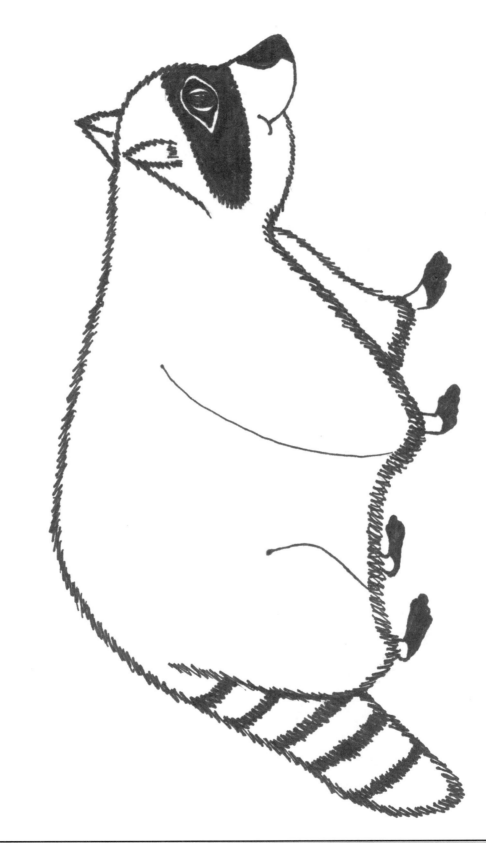

Figure 2.44 Raccoon Pattern for "Wake Up Bear"

Figure 2.45 Mouse and Rabbit Patterns for "Wake Up Bear"

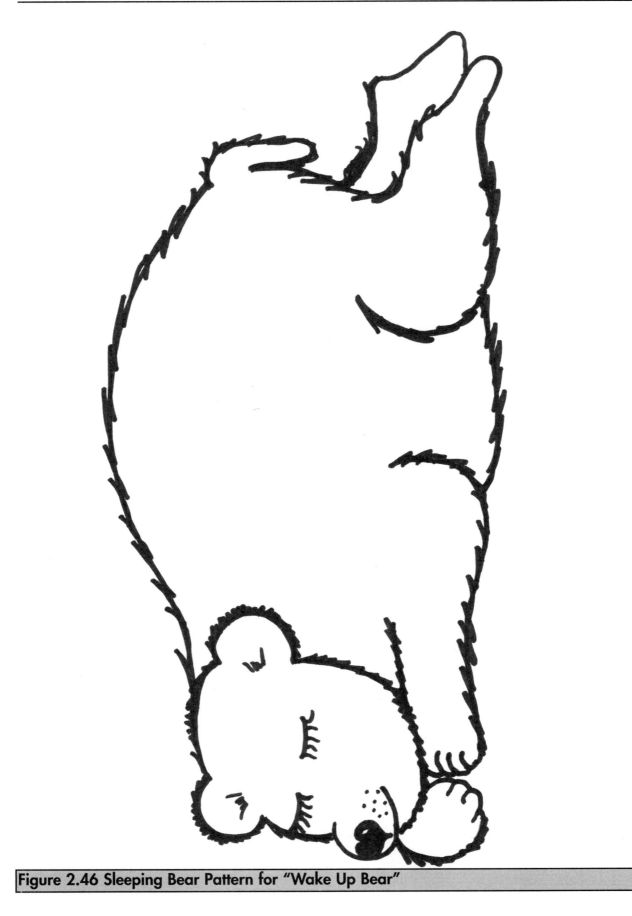

Figure 2.46 Sleeping Bear Pattern for "Wake Up Bear"

Figure 2.47 Laughing Bear Pattern for "Wake Up Bear"

Nuts

Seed

Grass

Squirrel

Figure 2.48 Nuts, Seed, Grass, and Squirrel Patterns for "Wake Up Bear"

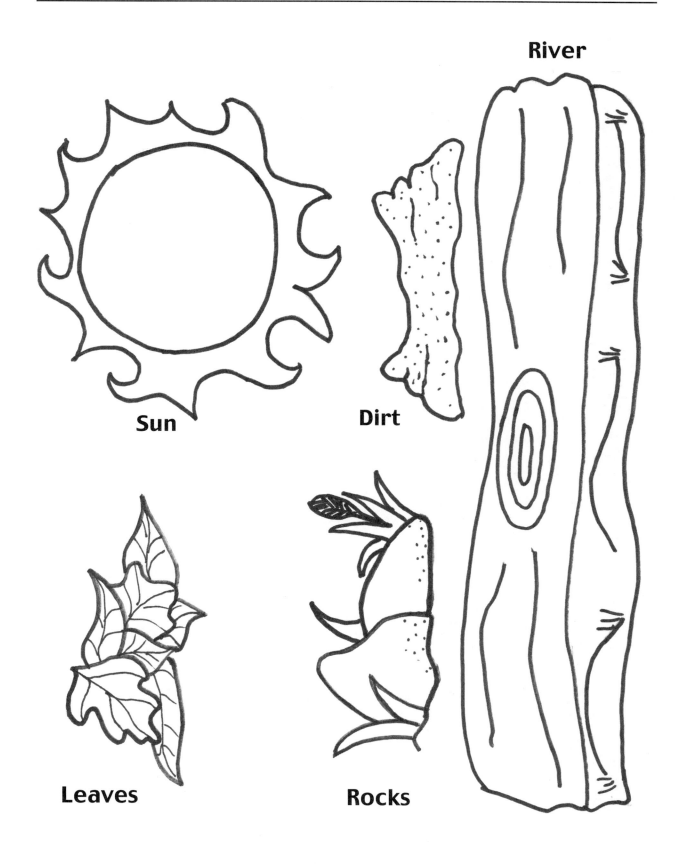

River

Sun

Dirt

Leaves

Rocks

Figure 2.49 Sun, Dirt, Leaves, Rocks, and River Patterns for "Wake Up Bear"

Spring Fling

Description

Spring Fling will allow preschoolers to blossom indoors in a large room or outdoors, weather permitting. This hour-long program is blooming with interactive stories and crafts. Celebrate spring with children and their parents and caregivers. Detailed craft and story instructions and patterns ensure success for this colorful event. Little ones and their parents will enjoy creating springtime masterpieces as they move from station to station, at the sound of a wind chime.

Publicity Page

Ready-to-personalize flyers are provided to make advertising your program a snap. To personalize use the CD ROM or simply cut and paste your program information onto the master and then reproduce. Enlarge and color your flyer to create an eye-catching poster for display.

(see Figure 3.1 on page 137)

Certificate

Easy-to-make certificates are wonderful keepsakes for parents and caregivers. Certificates may be handed out at the conclusion of your program (best for small crowds), or simply placed at a table for parents and caregivers to help themselves.

To create certificates you will need enough paper so that each participant receives one.

To Make Certificates:

1. Use CD ROM and print, type, or cut and paste your library name, logo, date, library director's or mayor's signature, or other information onto certificate pattern.
2. Copy enough certificates—one for each child.

(see Figure 3.2 on page 138)

Bookmarks

Three whimsical bookmarks to color may be reproduced and given at any time during your program. You may also choose to distribute them prior to your event, along with the publicity flyer, as a form of advertisement.

(see Figures 3.3, 3.4, 3.5 on pages 139 to 141)

Station Signs

Station signs identify activities in which children and their parents and caregivers may participate. Spring Fling was designed to include nine "craft" stations and one "storytime" station. Assign the storytime station the number one, as all participants will begin at this station, and then assign all other stations a random number. Divide participants into nine small groups and assign each a beginning station number.

To create station signs, you will need the following items:

- ten pieces of paper or cardstock
- laminate or clear contact paper (enough to cover signs)
- tape

To Make Signs:

1. Reproduce one sign for each station.
2. Color signs.
3. Laminate or cover signs with clear contact paper.
4. Tape station signs on wall or other visible location near each station.
5. Be sure to cover all station tables with a protective covering (paper, plastic tablecloth, etc.).

   NOTE: Laminated signs may be used year after year.

   (see Figures 3.6, 3.7, 3.8, 3.9, 3.10, 3.11, 3.12, 3.13, 3.14, 3.15 on pages 142 to 151)

Craft Activities

The following craft patterns with instructions are provided for you:

- Baggie Butterfly Craft *(on page 125)*
- Barnyard Hideaway Search and Color Page *(on page 126)*
- Chick in the Egg Craft *(on page 126)*
- Garden Rock Ornament Craft *(on page 126 to 127)*
- Glitzy Sunglasses Craft *(on page 127)*
- Pinecone Bird Feeder Craft *(on page 127 to 128)*
- Sun Visor Craft *(on page 128)*
- Tissue Paper Bee Craft *(on page 128 to 129)*
- Wormy Apple Craft *(on page 129)*

Baggie Butterfly Craft

Butterflies are always a welcome sign of spring. Children will love this see-through version of a butterfly made from a baggie.

To create this craft, you will need the following items:

- Baggie brand sandwich bags without zip top (one for each butterfly)
- black or brown pipe cleaners (one for each butterfly)
- small pieces of colored paper (or confetti)
- Scotch tape

To Make Baggie Butterfly:

1. Place small paper pieces or confetti into baggie and tape end shut.
2. Fold the pipe cleaner in half.
3. Gather middle of baggie, making sure that paper pieces or confetti are evenly distributed.
4. Place baggie between pipe cleaner and twist into place.
5. Continue twisting to form a body, leaving a small loop for finger.
6. Use remaining ends to form antenna.

   OPTIONAL: Use butterfly with "Butterfly Song."

Butterfly! Butterfly! Song

The "Butterfly! Butterfly!" is the perfect companion to the "Baggie Butterfly." Musical score is also provided.

(Play number five from CD. Using butterflies, created during craft time, have participants stand in circle, facing in, and follow the words, as your butterfly dances from place to place.)

Butterfly, butterfly, where did you go?
(Butterfly flutters in front of self.)
Fly up high and then down low.
(Butterfly flies up and then down.)
Butterfly, butterfly, where can you be?
(Butterfly flutters in front of self.)
Behind my back where I can't see.
(Butterfly flies behind back.)
Butterfly, butterfly, what did you hear?
(Butterfly flutters in front of self.)
Fluttering wings land on my ear.
(Butterfly flies to ear.)
Butterfly, butterfly, feel the wind blow.
(Butterfly flutters in front of self.)
Now you've landed on my toe.
(Butterfly flies to toe.)

Butterfly, butterfly, be on your way,
  (Butterfly flutters in front of self.)
Come back soon another day.
  (Butterfly flies behind back.)
        (see Figure 3.16 on page 152)

Barnyard Hideaway Search and Color Page

A search and find page fun for any age. Parents are encouraged to assist the little ones as they search for a hidden peanut, donut, toothbrush, flag, and baseball bat. When all the hidden items are found, enjoy coloring them and the rest of the page.

To create this color page craft, you will need the following items: crayons and enough paper to provide one sheet for each participant.

To Make Barnyard Hideaway:

1. Reproduce one Barnyard Hideaway for each participant from pattern provided.
2. Supply crayons and an area for children to color.

    (see Figure 3.17 on page 153)

Chick in the Egg Craft

This simple craft will delight children as the chick "hatches" from an egg.

To create this craft, you will need the following items:

- cardstock (one piece each of yellow and white)
- scissors
- one small brass brad for each participant
- patterns

To Make Chick in the Egg Craft:

1. Reproduce enough chicks, on yellow cardstock, and eggs, on white cardstock, for each participant.
2. Cut out patterns.
3. Connect egg pieces by placing brad through paper marked by dot.
4. Place chick behind connected egg pieces.
5. Place brad through chick and fasten.

    OPTIONAL: You may choose to provide a copy of the words for each child.
    (see Figures 3.18, 3.19 on pages 154 to 155)

Garden Rock Ornament Craft

Garden Rock Ornaments will add a bright spot to any corner of the garden.

To create this craft, you will need the following items:

- smooth rocks of varying shapes (enough for each participant)
- craft-size paintbrushes

- disposable containers for water
- paper towels
- nontoxic paint (in a variety of colors)
- spray fixative (any type—optional)

To Make a Garden Rock Ornament:

1. Wash and dry all rocks.
2. Place all supplies on craft table.
3. Encourage children to create something for their garden. You may want to provide samples such as an animal painted on a rock, a plain brightly-colored rock, etc.

   OPTIONAL: A hairdryer will help dry these garden treasures, in the event your spring fling is conducted indoors on a cloudy day!

Glitzy Sunglasses Craft

Designer glasses are a must for any springtime outfit!
To create this craft, you will need the following items:

- cardstock to reproduce enough glasses patterns (one for each participant)
- white glue
- glitter
- sequins
- lace scraps (in other words, clean out those craft supply drawers!)
- scissors
- pipe cleaners (enough to provide two for each pair of glasses)

To Make Glitzy Sunglasses:

1. Reproduce glasses pattern.
2. Encourage parents and caregivers to assist young children in cutting pattern and decorating glasses.

   (see Figure 3.20 on page 156)

Pinecone Bird Feeder Craft

Calling all birds! Children will enjoy creating this environmentally-friendly bird feeder.
To create this craft, you will need the following items:

- pinecones (one for each participant)
- smooth peanut butter (approximately 1/2 cup per pine cone)
- craft sticks (one for each participant)
- yarn (approximately 12 inches for each bird feeder)
- ziplock bags (one for each bird feeder)
- birdseed (approximately 1/4 cup per feeder)

To Make Pinecone Bird Feeder:

1. Tie yarn around top of pinecone.
2. Using craft stick, spread peanut butter on outside edges of pinecones.
3. Sprinkle birdseed onto peanut butter.
4. Place in ziplock bag.

    OPTIONAL: You may want to premeasure peanut butter into small disposable paper cups and place a craft stick in each cup.

Sun Visor Craft

Children will love decorating a sun visor to wear on a sunny spring day.
To create this craft, you will need the following items:

- visor patterns
- cardstock in a variety of colors
- crayons
- colored pencils (or markers)
- string (or rubber bands or thin elastic strips)
- hole punch

To Make a Sun Visor:

1. Reproduce, color, and cut out patterns—one for each participant.
2. Punch holes marked by dots.
3. Attach string (or rubber band or elastic) to holes.

OPTIONAL: Visors can be made from colorful craft foam.

(see Figures 3.21, 3.22, 3.23 on pages 157 to 159)

Tissue Paper Bee Craft

Parents will enjoy helping to make tissue paper bees come alive, as their children create textured stripes on a friendly bee.
To create this craft, you will need the following items:

- bee pattern
- yellow cardstock
- yellow and black tissue paper (approximately 1/4 sheet of each to make one bee)
- white glue
- scissors
- a few unsharpened pencils

To Make Tissue Paper Bee:

1. Reproduce bee patterns—one for each participant.
2. Cut yellow and black tissue paper into small 1 x 1-inch squares. (These don't need to be precise) and best if prepared ahead of time.

3. Spread a thin layer of glue onto first bee stripe.
4. Wrap one piece of black tissue paper loosely around the pencil eraser.
5. Tip pencil and touch tissue paper to glue, and then remove pencil. (Tissue paper will stick.)
6. Repeat above step, placing tissue pieces very close together covering entire stripe.
7. Spread glue on next stripe and repeat steps 4 and 5 using yellow tissue paper.
8. Alternate stripes until all stripes are filled.

   (see Figure 3.24 on page 160)

Wormy Apple Craft

The only apple that truly welcomes a worm! Yarn worms can munch their way through a juicy red apple over and over again!

To create this craft, you will need the following items:

- apple pattern
- red cardstock (or tag board)
- green yarn (6-inch lengths—one for each apple)
- hole punch
- Scotch tape

1. Reproduce apple patterns—one for each child.
2. Punch holes in apple marked by dots.
3. Tightly wrap a small piece of Scotch tape around one end of yarn.
4. Instruct children to "thread" the worm through the holes in the apple.

   OPTIONAL: If time allows, conduct "worm races."

   (see Figure 3.25 on page 161)

Stories

The following stories and patterns are provided for you:

Chick in the Egg

(After telling this short story, let children know that they will be making a Chick in the Egg of their very own!)

I have a little egg,

   (Hold up egg.)

but it's not mine to keep.

(Shake head "no.")
'Cuz out popped a chick
   (Open egg to reveal chick.)
that went, "Peep, peep, peep!"
   (Make peeping noise.)

To Make as a Prop Story:

1. Reproduce chick on yellow cardstock and egg on white cardstock.
2. Cut out patterns.
3. Connect egg pieces by placing brad through paper marked by dot.
4. Place chick behind connected egg pieces.
5. Place brad through chick and fasten.

(see Figures 3.26, 3.27 on pages 162 to 163)

Grandma, Grandma Look and See

(Before you begin, place flowers on flannel board and say with excitement:)
Grandma! Grandma! Look and see…
I brought a butterfly home with me!
   (Hold flannel butterfly up for all to see and then hold it, cupped in hands.)
Grandma said we should let wild things be,
So I set my beautiful butterfly free.
   (Place butterfly on board near flowers.)
Grandma! Grandma! Look and see…
I brought an inchworm home with me!
   (Hold flannel inchworm up for all to see and then hold it, cupped in hands.)
Grandma said we should let wild things be,
So I set my cute inchworm free!
   (Place inchworm on board under flowers.)
Grandma! Grandma! Look and see…
I brought a songbird home with me!
   (Hold flannel bird up for all to see and then hold it, cupped in hands.)
Grandma said we should let wild things be,
So I set my lovely songbird free!
   (Place bird on board above flowers.)
Grandma! Grandma! Look and see…
I brought a slimy frog home with me!
   (Hold flannel worm up for all to see and then hold it, cupped in hands.)
Grandma said we should let wild things be,
So I set my slimy little froggy free!
   (Place frog on board near flowers.)
Grandma! Grandma! Look and see…

Daddy brought a cuddly kitten home for me!
  (Hold flannel kitten up for all to see and then hold it, cupped in hands.)
Grandma said she was beautiful, and I must agree;
Looks like the perfect pet for me!
  (Smile and hug kitten.)

  OPTIONAL: Use stuffed animals or puppets.

To Make as a Flannel Story:

1. Cut all patterns from felt in colors of your choice.
2. Enhance with felt markers.

  (see Figures 3.28, 3.29, 3.30, 3.31, 3.32, 3.33 on pages 164 to 169)

To Make as a Magnetic Story:

1. Reproduce patterns.
2. Color all patterns in colors of your choice.
3. Laminate patterns.
4. Cut out patterns.
5. Attach a magnetic strip to the back of each piece.

  (see Figures 3.28, 3.29, 3.30, 3.31, 3.32, 3.33 on pages 164 to 169)

Here Is the Nest for Bluebird

Here is the nest
  (Place nest on flannel board.)
for Bluebird;
  (Place Bluebird in nest.)
Here is the hive
  (Place hive on flannel board.)
for Bee;
  (Place Bee on hive.)
Here is the hole
  (Place hole on flannel board.)
for Bunny;
  (Place Bunny on hole.)
And here is the house
  (Place house on flannel board.)
for me!
  (Point to self.)

To Make as a Flannel Story:

1. Cut all patterns from felt in colors of your choice, unless otherwise indicated in story.
2. Enhance with felt markers.

  (see Figures 3.34, 3.35, 3.36, 3.37, 3.38 on pages 170 to 174)

To Make as a Magnetic Story:

1. Reproduce patterns.
2. Color all patterns in colors of your choice, unless otherwise indicated in story.
3. Laminate patterns.
4. Cut out patterns.
5. Attach a magnetic strip to the back of each piece.

   (see Figures 3.34, 3.35, 3.36, 3.37, 3.38 on pages 170 to 174)

Little Rabbit and the Vegetable Garden

(Play number six from CD.)

Little Rabbit was not allowed to go into the farmer's vegetable garden. His mama had told him not to. Oh, but that lettuce is so crisp, and the carrots so crunchy. He couldn't help himself. He swished through the grassy meadow.

   (Rub palms of hands together to make a swishing sound.)

He hopped over the rocks around the field.

   (Slap both hands on thighs five times.)

He wriggled under the fence around the garden.

   (Bend over at waist and wiggle shoulders back and forth.)

And he tiptoed through the water in the rows around the vegetables.

   (Place hands with palms face down, make a loose fist, and then alternate moving hands up and down to resemble tiptoeing.)

Finally he was face to face with a big green head of lettuce. Just as he was about to take a great big bite, he heard, "Silly rabbit, don't make this a habit. Get out of my garden!"

Little Rabbit tiptoed though the water as fast as he could.

   (Place hands with palms face down, make a loose fist, and then alternate moving hands quickly up and down to resemble tiptoeing.)

He wriggled quickly under the fence around the garden.

   (Bend over at waist and quickly wiggle shoulders back and forth.)

He hopped quickly over the rocks around the field.

   (Quickly slap both hands on thighs five times.)

He swished through the grassy meadow back to his home.

   (Quickly rub palms of hands together to make a swishing sound.)

Little Rabbit stopped and panted, "Wow, that was close, I ALMOST got a bite!" Oh, but that lettuce is so crisp, and the carrots so crunchy. Even though his mama had told him not to, he couldn't help himself. "I'm not scared!" said Little Rabbit as he swished through the grassy meadow.

   (Rub palms of hands together to make a swishing sound.)

He hopped over the rocks around the field.

   (Slap both hands on thighs five times.)

He wriggled under the fence around the garden.

   (Bend over at waist and wiggle shoulders back and forth.)

And he tiptoed through the water in the rows around the vegetables.

(Place hands palms face down, make a loose fist, and then alternate moving hands up and down to resemble tiptoeing.)

Finally he was face to face with a crunchy orange carrot. Just as he was about to take a great big bite, he heard, "Silly rabbit, don't make this a habit. Get out of my garden!"

Little Rabbit tiptoed though the water as fast as he could.

(Place hands with palms face down, make a loose fist, and then alternate moving hands quickly up and down.)

He wriggled quickly under the fence around the garden.

(Bend over at waist and quickly wiggle shoulders back and forth.)

He hopped quickly over the rocks around the field.

(Quickly slap both hands on thighs five times.)

He swished through the grassy meadow back to his home.

(Quickly rub palms of hands together to make a swishing sound.)

Suddenly Little Rabbit stopped and thought, "Wait a minute, I didn't see the farmer." Oh, but that lettuce is so crisp, and the carrots so crunchy". that Even though his mama had told him not to, he couldn't help himself. "I'm not scared!" thought Little Rabbit as he swished through the grassy meadow.

(Rub palms of hands together to make a swishing sound.)

He hopped over the rocks around the field.

(Slap both hands on thighs five times.)

This time Little Rabbit stopped at the garden fence. He looked around for the farmer.

(Slowly turn head from side to side.)

He didn't see the farmer; so he wriggled under the fence around the garden.

(Bend over at waist and wiggle shoulders back and forth,)

Little Rabbit stopped and looked around for the farmer.

No farmer—so he tiptoed through the water in the rows around the vegetables.

(Place hands palms face down, make a loose fist, and then alternate moving hands up and down to resemble tiptoeing.)

Finally he was face to face with a crunchy orange carrot, but just as he was about to take a great big bite, he heard, "Silly rabbit, don't make this a habit. Get out of my garden!"

But Little Rabbit didn't run, he hunched down and looked around. There was a pole in the ground. He looked way up to the top of the pole. There sat a beautiful green bird who kept saying, "Silly rabbit, don't make this a habit. Get out of my garden!"

(Hold up paint stick with parrot on top.)

Little Rabbit stood up straight and smiled to himself, as he held up the crunchy orange carrot and said, "Silly parrot, I'm going to eat this carrot." Hee Hee

To Prepare for This Story:

1. Reproduce parrot pattern.
2. Color pattern.
3. Laminate pattern.
4. Attach pattern to paint stick.

   (see Figure 3.39 on page 175)

Roadrunner's Surprise

(This story can be sung to the tune "Head, Shoulder, Knees, and Toes." Before you begin, place all pieces on the magnetic board [except Roadrunner]. Put the snake behind the rock, the crow behind the cloud, the owl behind the tree, the mouse behind the hill, and the girl roadrunner behind the cactus.)

Slow down, Roadrunner. Why must you run so fast?

(Run in place.)

Slow down, Roadrunner. Did you see what you just passed?

(Shade eyes with hand.)

Behind that rock, a snake was slithering there.

(Point to rock, remove rock, and give children opportunity to say "snake.")

Slow down, Roadrunner, if you dare. If you dare!

Slow down, Roadrunner. Why must you run so fast?

(Run in place.)

Slow down, Roadrunner. Did you see what you just passed?

(Shade eyes with hand.)

Behind that cloud, a crow was flying there.

(Point to cloud, remove cloud, and give children opportunity to say "crow" or "bird.")

Slow down, Roadrunner, if you dare. If you dare!

Slow down, Roadrunner. Why must you run so fast?

(Run in place.)

Slow down, Roadrunner. Did you see what you just passed?

(Shade eyes with hand.)

Behind that tree, an owl was hooting there.

(Point to tree, remove tree, and give children opportunity to say "owl.")

Slow down, Roadrunner, if you dare. If you dare!

Slow down, Roadrunner. Why must you run so fast?

(Run in place.)

Slow down, Roadrunner. Did you see what you just passed?

(Shade eyes with hand.)

Behind that hill, a mouse was hiding there.

(Point to hill, remove hill, and give children opportunity to say "mouse.")

Slow down, Roadrunner, if you dare. If you dare!

Slow down, Roadrunner. Why must you run so fast?

(Run in place.)

Slow down, Roadrunner. Did you see what you just passed?

(Shade eyes with hand.)

Behind that cactus, I was waiting there.

(Point to cactus, remove cactus, and point to girl roadrunner.)

Slow down, Roadrunner, if you dare. ' 'Cuz (darn creative license!) I care!

To Make as a Magnetic Story:

1. Reproduce patterns.
2. Color all patterns in colors of your choice.
3. Laminate patterns.
4. Cut out patterns.
5. Attach a magnetic strip to the back of each piece.

   (see Figures 3.40, 3.41, 3.42, 3.43, 3.44, 3.45, 3.46 on pages 176 to 182)

The Seed Story

This is the garden at my house.
  (Point to flannel board.)
  (Place seed at center of flannel board)
This is the seed that I planted
in the garden at my house.
  (Place rain in top left corner of flannel board.)
This is the rain
that fell on the seed that I planted
in the garden at my house.
  (Place sun in top right corner of flannel board)
This is the sun
that dried up the rain
that fell on the seed that I planted
in the garden at my house.
  (Place root under [and touching] seed on flannel board.)
This is the root
that grew down deep
when the sun dried up the rain
that fell on the seed that I planted
in the garden at my house.
  (Place stem at top [and touching] seed on flannel board.)
This is the stem
that grew up straight
while the root grew down deep
when the sun dried up the rain
that fell on the seed that I planted
in the garden at my house.
  (Place bud at top [and touching] stem on flannel board.)
This is the bud
that formed on the stem
that grew up straight
while the root grew down deep

when the sun dried up the rain
that fell on the seed that I planted
in the garden at my house.
  (Place flower over [and covering] bud on flannel board.)
This is the flower
that opened from the bud
that formed on the stem
that grew up straight
while the root grew down deep
when the sun dried up the rain
that fell on the seed that I planted
in the garden at my house.
This is me, enjoying the flower.
  (Point to self and then smell flower.)

To Make as a Flannel Story:

1. Cut all patterns from felt in colors of your choice, unless otherwise indicated in story.
2. Enhance with felt markers.
   (see Figures 3.47, 3.48, 3.49, 3.50 on pages 183 to 186)

To Make as a Magnetic Story:

1. Reproduce patterns.
2. Color all patterns in colors of your choice, unless otherwise indicated in story.
3. Laminate patterns.
4. Cut out patterns.
5. Attach a magnetic strip to the back of each piece.
   (see Figures 3.47, 3.48, 3.49, 3.50 on pages 183 to 186)

Spring Fling Support Materials

Spring Fling Support Materials run from pages 137 to 186.

Figure 3.1 Publicity Page for "Spring Fling"

Figure 3.2 Certificate for "Spring Fling"

Figure 3.3 "Read" Bookmark

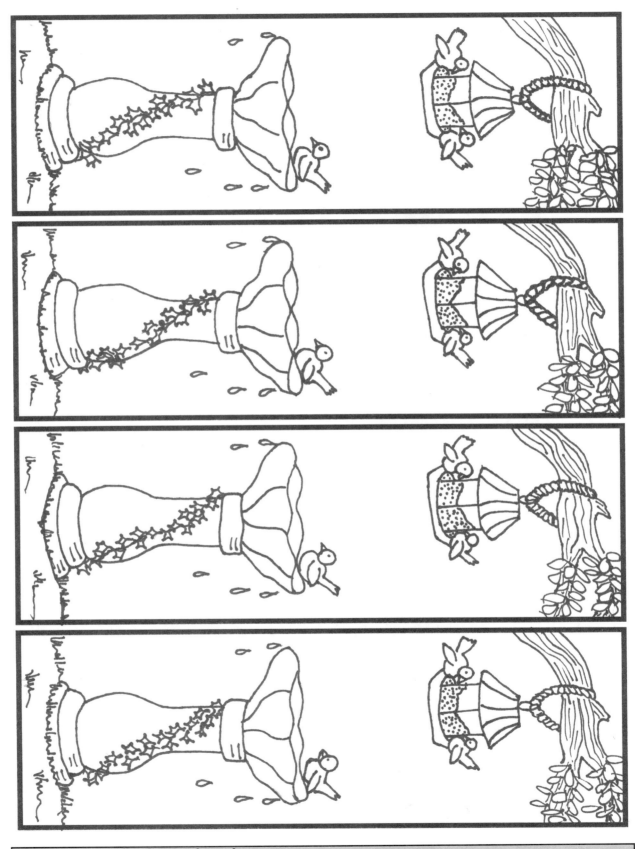

Figure 3.4 "Birdbath" Bookmark

Figure 3.5 "Sunflower" Bookmark

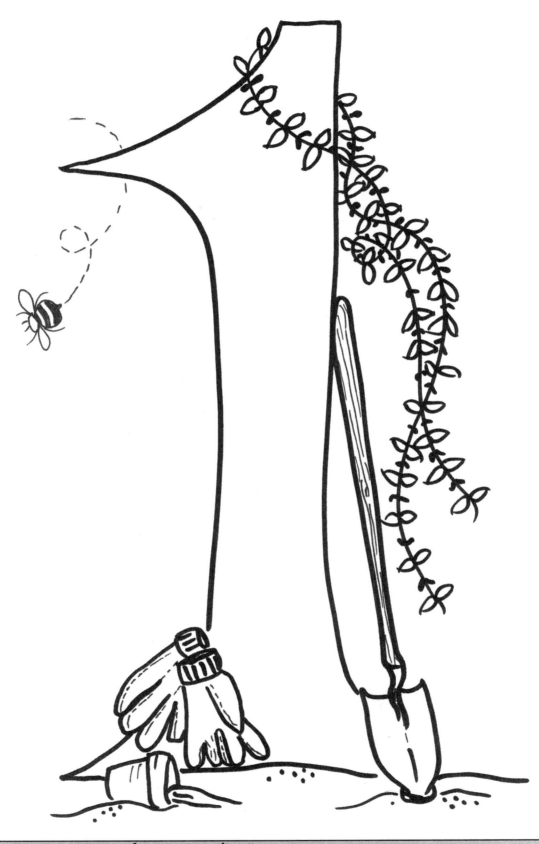

Figure 3.6 Station Sign for "Spring Fling"

Figure 3.7 Station Sign for "Spring Fling"

Figure 3.8 Station Sign for "Spring Fling"

Figure 3.9 Station Sign for "Spring Fling"

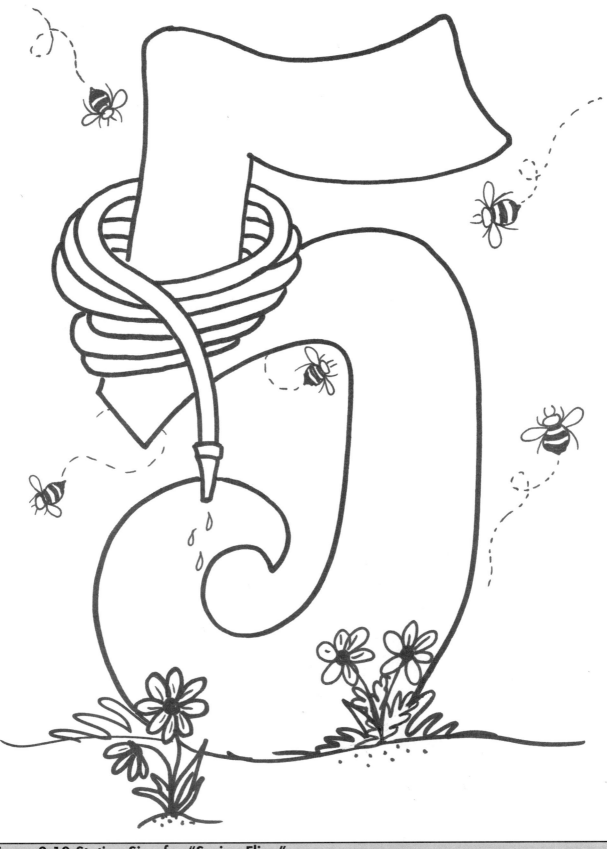

Figure 3.10 Station Sign for "Spring Fling"

Figure 3.11 Station Sign for "Spring Fling"

Figure 3.12 Station Sign for "Spring Fling"

Figure 3.13 Station Sign for "Spring Fling"

Figure 3.14 Station Sign for "Spring Fling"

Figure 3.15 Station Sign for "Spring Fling"

Figure 3.16 Musical Score for "Butterfly! Butterfly! Song"

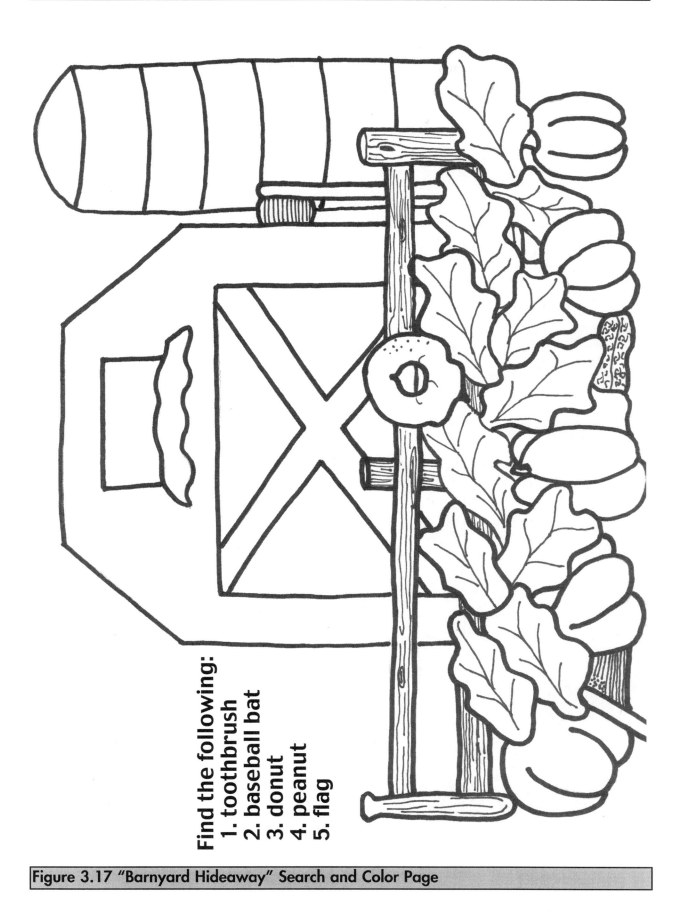

Find the following:
1. toothbrush
2. baseball bat
3. donut
4. peanut
5. flag

Figure 3.17 "Barnyard Hideaway" Search and Color Page

Figure 3.18 Chick Pattern for "Chick in the Egg Craft"

Figure 3.19 Egg Pattern for "Chick in the Egg Craft"

- **Cut sunglass patterns from cardstock**
- **punch holes—indicated by O**
- **decorate**
- **attach pipe cleaners through holes to create earpieces**

Figure 3.20 Pattern for "Glitzy Sunglasses Craft"

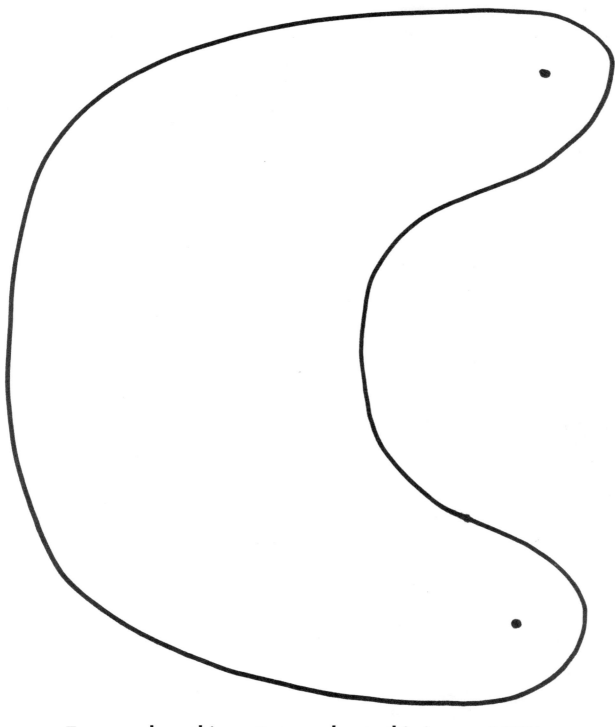

To reproduce this pattern, enlarge this image 130%.

Figure 3.21 Blank Visor Pattern for "Sun Visor Craft"

To reproduce this pattern, enlarge this image 130%.

Figure 3.22 Frog Visor Pattern for "Sun Visor Craft"

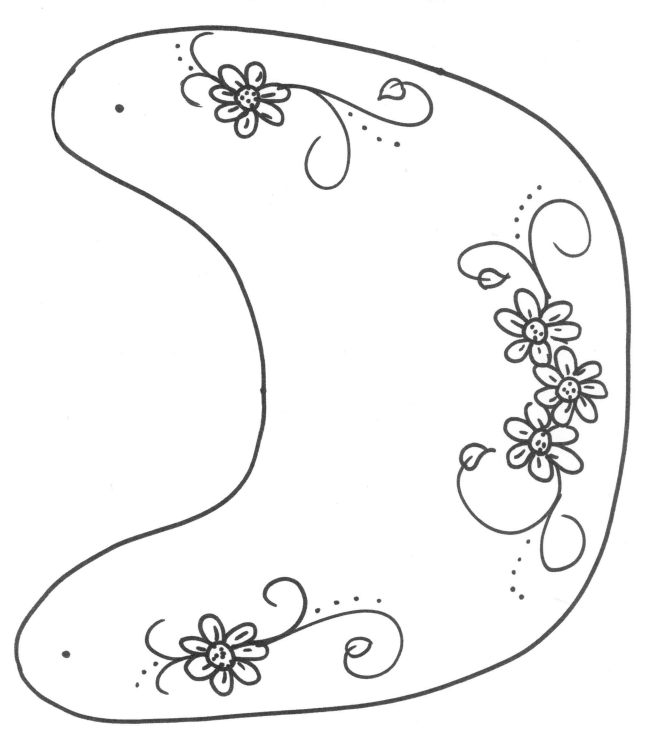

To reproduce this pattern, enlarge this image 130%.

Figure 3.23 Spring Visor Pattern for "Sun Visor Craft"

Figure 3.24 Bee Pattern for "Tissue Paper Bee Craft"

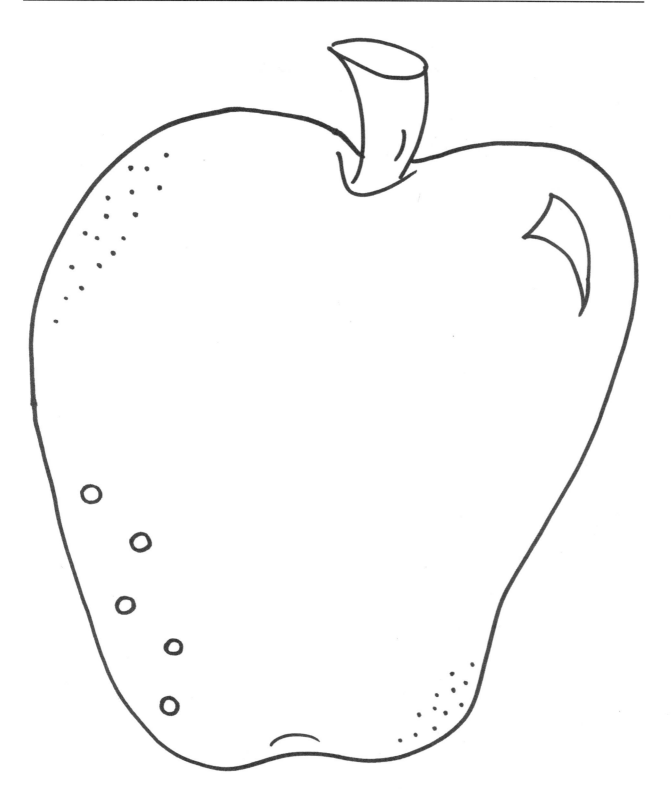

Figure 3.25 Apple Pattern for "Wormy Apple Craft"

Figure 3.26 Chick Pattern for "Chick in the Egg Story"

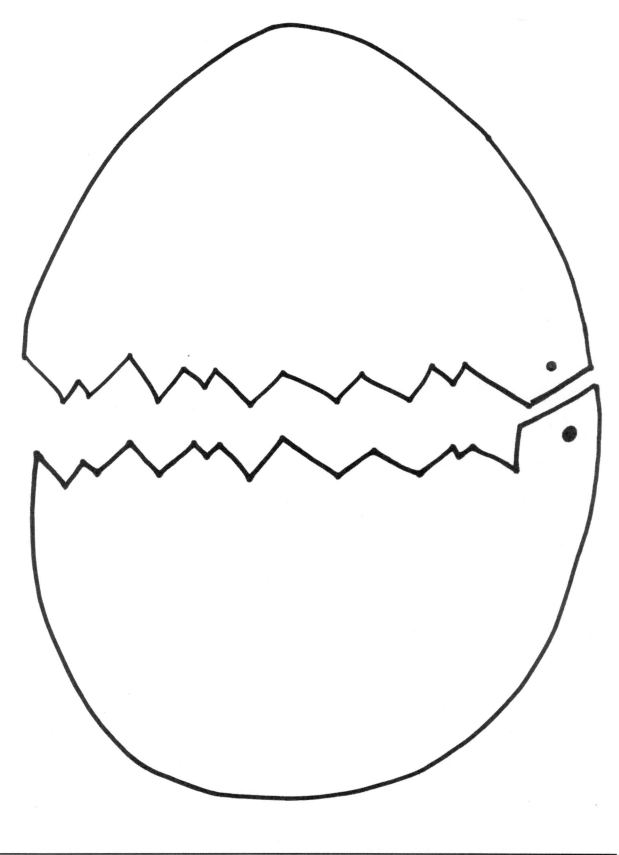

Figure 3.27 Egg Pattern for "Chick in the Egg Story"

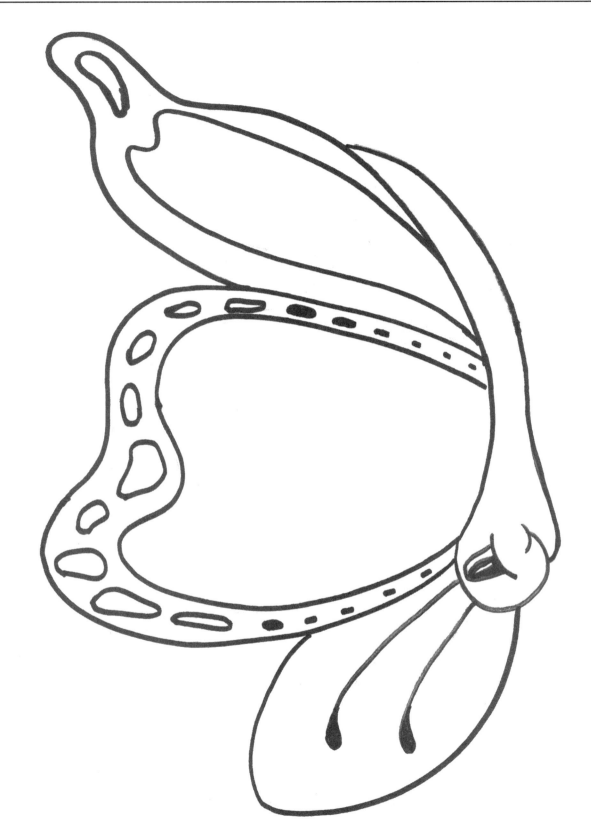

Figure 3.28 Butterfly Pattern for "Grandma, Grandma Look and See"

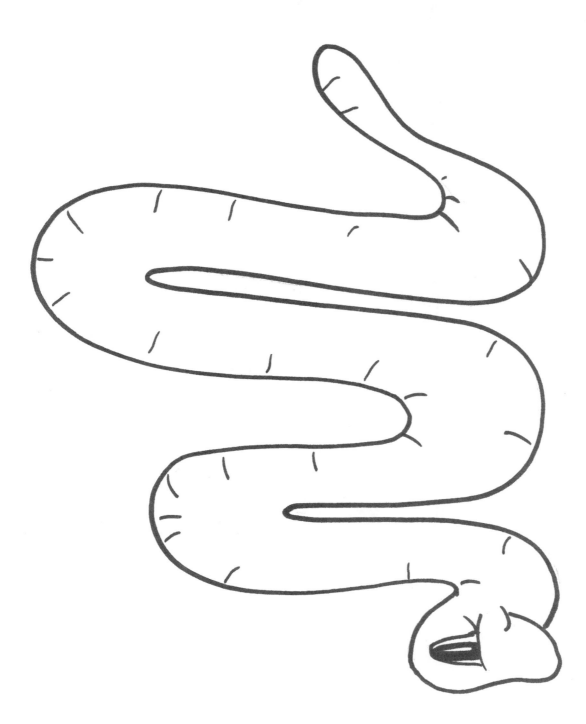

Figure 3.29 Inchworm Pattern for "Grandma, Grandma Look and See"

Figure 3.30 Bird Pattern for "Grandma, Grandma Look and See"

Figure 3.31 Frog Pattern for "Grandma, Grandma Look and See"

Figure 3.32 Cat Pattern for "Grandma, Grandma Look and See"

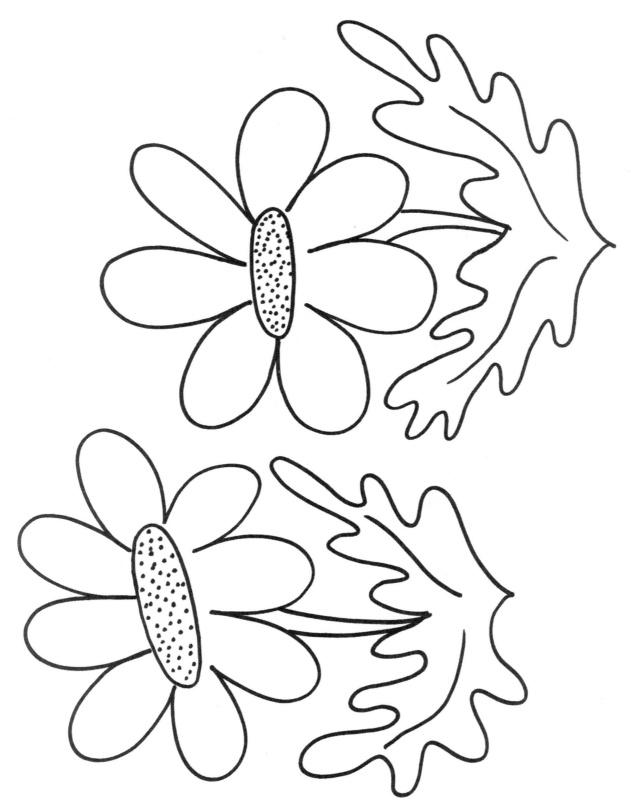

Reproduce two times for a total of four flowers

Figure 3.33 Flower Patterns for "Grandma, Grandma Look and See"

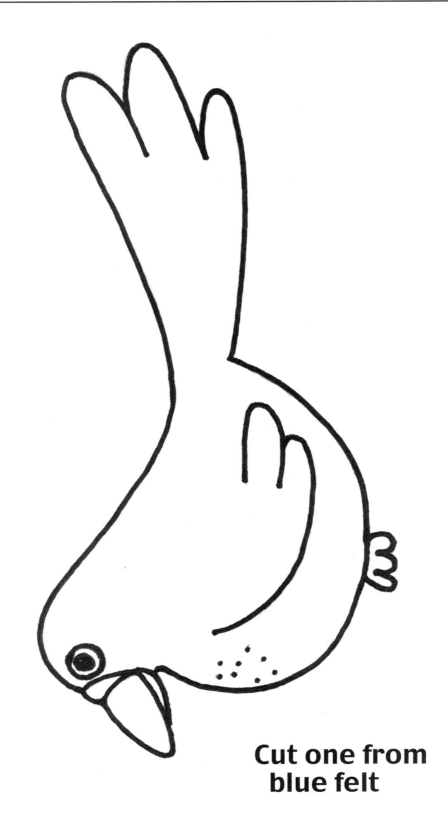

Cut one from blue felt

Figure 3.34 Bluebird Pattern for "Here is the Nest for Bluebird"

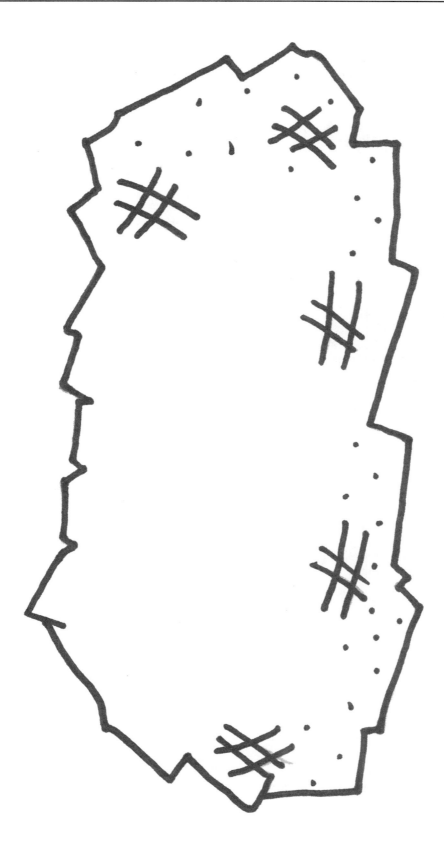

Figure 3.35 Nest Pattern for "Here is the Nest for Bluebird"

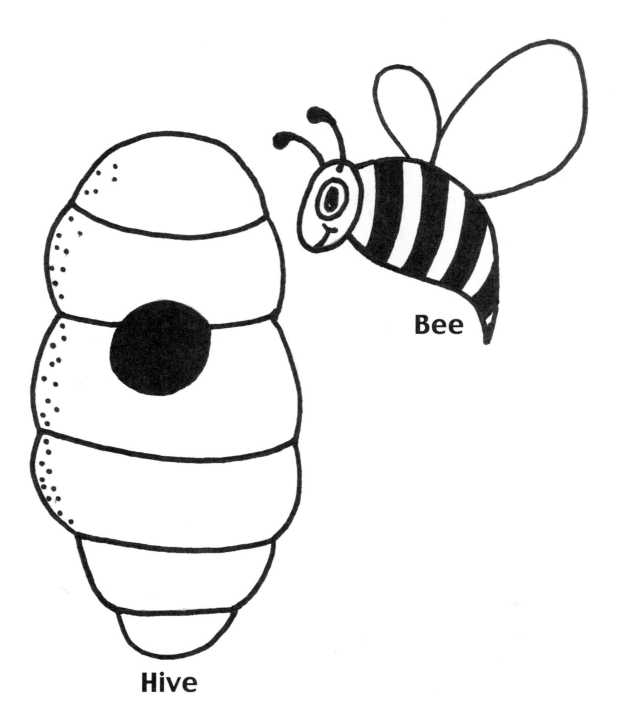

Bee

Hive

Figure 3.36 Bee and Hive Patterns for "Here is the Nest for Bluebird"

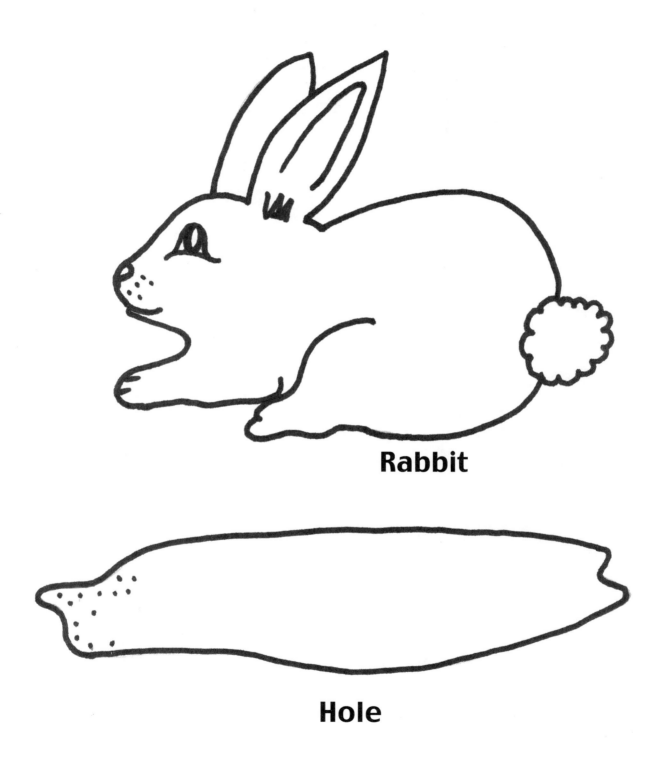

Rabbit

Hole

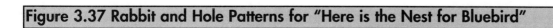

Figure 3.37 Rabbit and Hole Patterns for "Here is the Nest for Bluebird"

Figure 3.38 House Pattern for "Here is the Nest for Bluebird"

Figure 3.39 Parrot Pattern for "Little Rabbit and the Vegetable Garden"

Snake

Crow

Figure 3.40 Snake and Crow Patterns for "Roadrunner's Surprise"

Mouse

Owl

"Girl" Roadrunner

Figure 3.41 Mouse, Owl, and "Girl" Roadrunner Patterns for "Roadrunner's Surprise"

Figure 3.42 Tree Pattern for "Roadrunner's Surprise"

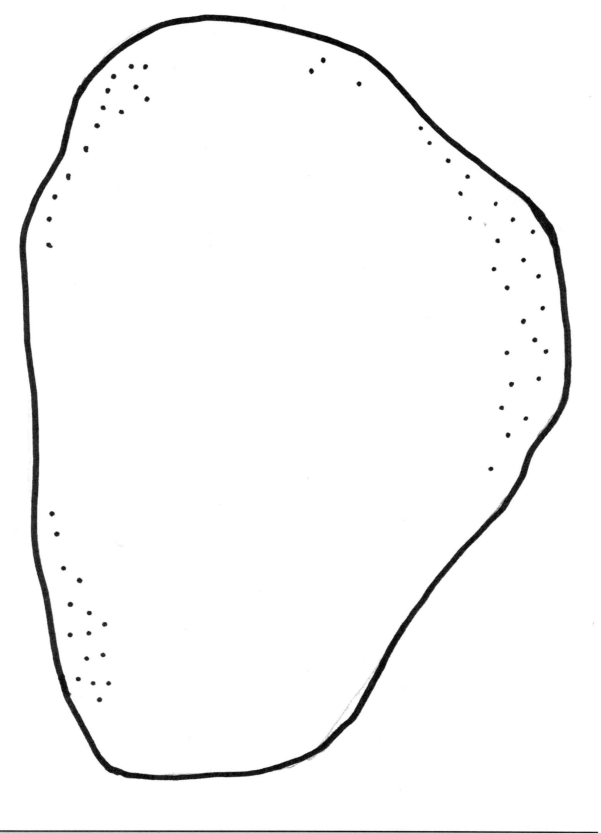

Figure 3.43 Rock Pattern for "Roadrunner's Surprise"

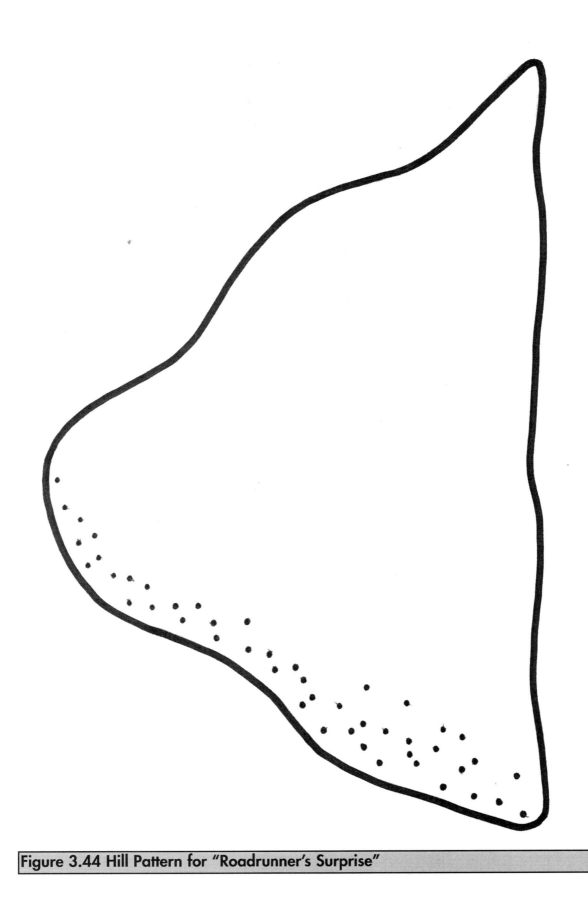

Figure 3.44 Hill Pattern for "Roadrunner's Surprise"

Figure 3.45 Cloud Pattern for "Roadrunner's Surprise"

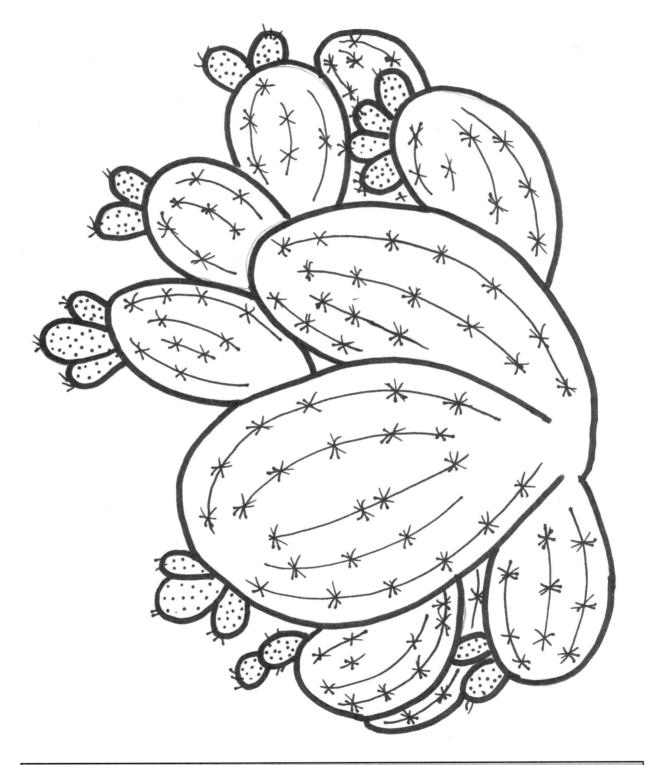

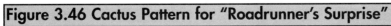

Figure 3.46 Cactus Pattern for "Roadrunner's Surprise"

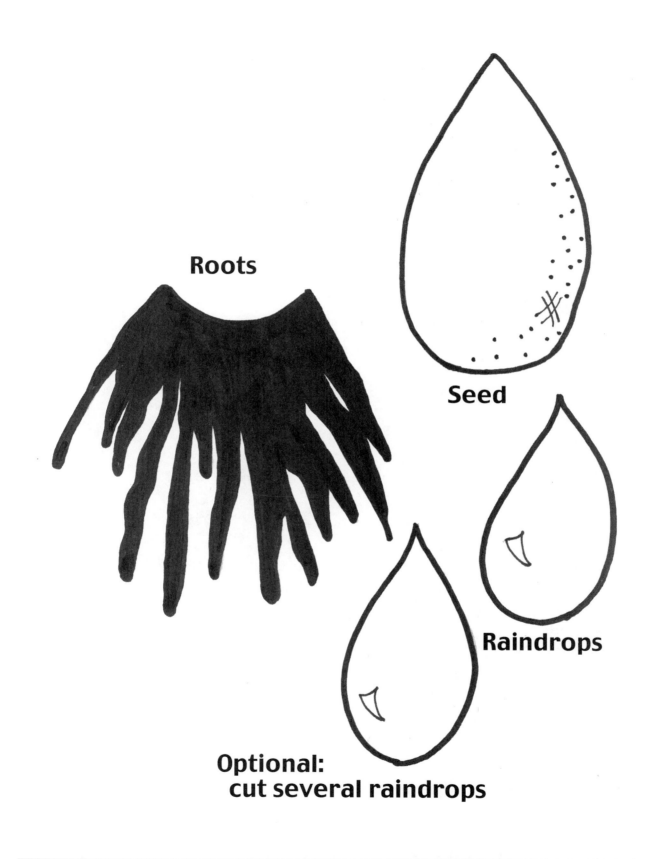

Roots

Seed

Raindrops

**Optional:
cut several raindrops**

Figure 3.47 Roots, Seed, and Raindrop Patterns for "The Seed Story"

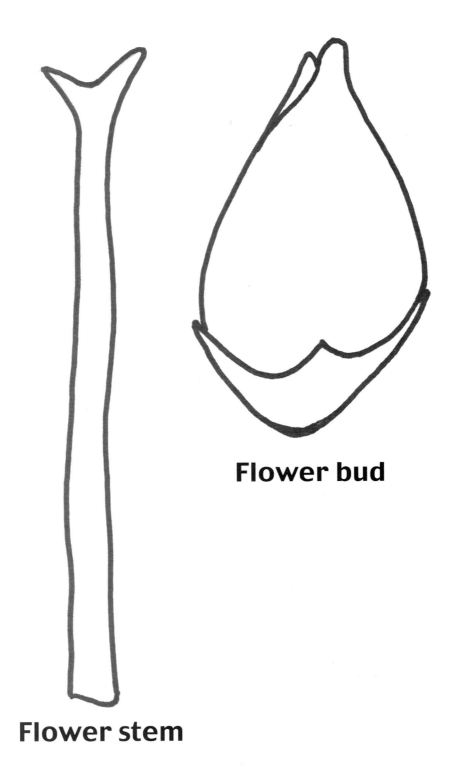

Flower bud

Flower stem

Figure 3.48 Flower Bud and Stem Patterns for "The Seed Story"

Figure 3.49 Flower Pattern for "The Seed Story"

Figure 3.50 Sun Pattern for "The Seed Story"

Seasonal Program 4

Halloween Boo

Description

Invite children and their parents and caregivers to wear a costume, listen to Halloween stories, and trick-or-treat in a safe environment. During this hour-long program, plan fifteen minutes for stories and forty-five minutes for a costume parade. Children can trick or treat through your library or school, collecting a variety of goodies. You may choose to provide drinks and treats at the end of the parade. To prepare for Halloween Boo, simply map out a parade route through your library or school and arrange for several volunteers and staff members to hand out goodies along the route. We have even provided a lively Halloween March for participants to enjoy as they parade from station to station.

Publicity Page

Ready-to-personalize flyers are provided to make advertising your program a snap. To personalize use the CD ROM or simply cut and paste your program information onto the master, and then reproduce. Enlarge and color your flyer to create an eye-catching poster for display.

(see Figure 4.1 on page 199)

Station Signs

A Halloween Boo station assignment form is provided along with a sample checklist. Copy the assignment sheet, fill in the blanks, and you're ready to go! Remember to supply a chair and table for each volunteer.

(see Figures 4.2 and 4.3 on pages 200 to 201)

Certificate

Easy-to-make certificates are wonderful keepsakes for parents and caregivers. Certificates may be handed out at the conclusion of your program (best for small crowds), or simply placed at a table for parents and caregivers to help themselves.

To create certificates you will need enough paper so that each participant receives one.

To Make Certificates:

1. Use CD ROM and print, type, or cut and paste your library name, logo, date, library director's or mayor's signature, or other information onto certificate pattern.
2. Copy enough certificates—one for each child.

(see Figure 4.4 on page 202)

Station Signs

Ten cute station signs, designed to guide participants along the parade route, are provided. To create station signs, you will need the following items:

- ten pieces of paper or cardstock
- laminate or clear contact paper (enough to cover signs)
- tape

To Make Signs:

1. Reproduce one sign for each station.
2. Color signs.
3. Laminate or cover signs with clear contact paper.
4. Tape station signs on wall or other visible location near each stop.

   NOTE: Laminated signs may be used year after year.

   (see Figures 4.5, 4.6, 4.7, 4.8, 4.9, 4.10, 4.11, 4.12, 4.13, 4.14 on pages 203 to 212)

Stories

The following stories and patterns are provided for you:

- Halloween at the Zoo *(on pages 188 to 190)*
- Halloween Countdown *(on page 190)*
- One Dark and Gloomy Night *(on pages 191 to 192)*
- The Perfect Pet *(on pages 193 to 194)*
- To Scare Away the Crows *(on pages 194 to 195)*

Halloween at the Zoo

(Before you begin this story, place transparencies with animal—Giraffe's spots on Giraffe, Zebra's stripes on Zebra, Lion's mane on Lion, and bath towel on Elephant's back.)

Every year the zoo celebrated Halloween. All of the children that visited that day dressed in costumes. Year after year Giraffe,

(Place Giraffe with spots on board.)

Zebra,

(Place Zebra with stripes on board.)

lion,

(Place Lion with mane on board.)

and Elephant

(Place Elephant with bath towel on board.)

watched the fun. Elephant had been at the zoo the longest. It had been almost nine years since he was born there. Elephant had been thinking all year about how fun it would be if he could wear a costume on Halloween. Then he had an idea. He could hardly wait to tell Giraffe, Zebra, and Lion. So he trumpeted his plan loudly enough so that they could hear.

(Trumpet like an Elephant.)

For the next few days, there was much excitement at the zoo, as it was decorated with brightly-colored lights.

(Place lights at top of board.)

The animals could hardly wait. Elephant, Zebra, Lion, and Giraffe were the most excited of all. When the zoo gates opened and all of the costumed children arrived, a big surprise was waiting. Elephant gave giraffe his favorite bath towel.

(Remove bath towel from Elephant.)

Giraffe quickly removed his spots

(Remove giraffe's spots.)

and then covered himself with Elephant's bath towel.

(Place ghost costume over Giraffe.)

Lion removed his beautiful mane

(Remove Lion's mane.)

and then slipped into Giraffe's spots.

(Place Lion's spots transparency on Lion.)

Zebra shook himself to remove his stripes

(Remove Zebra's stripes.)

and placed Lion's mane around his own neck.

(Place Zebra's mane transparency on Zebra.)

And Elephant—well, Elephant had the most fun of all. He stood proudly in his magnificent stripes!

(Place Elephant's stripes transparency on Elephant.)

It was the best Halloween ever!

To Make as a Magnetic Story:

1. Reproduce elephant pattern *(Figure 4.15 on page 213)* on gray paper.
2. Reproduce giraffe pattern *(Figure 4.16 on page 214)* on goldenrod paper.
3. Reproduce lion pattern *(Figure 4.17 on page 215)* on tan paper.
4. Reproduce zebra pattern *(Figure 4.18 on page 216)* on white paper.
5. Reproduce lion's and zebra's mane patterns *(Figure 4.19 on page 217)* on brown paper.
6. Reproduce giraffe's ghost costume and elephant's towel patterns *(Figure 4.20 on page 218)* on white paper.
7. Laminate patterns.
8. Cut out patterns.
9. Reproduce giraffe's spots, elephant's stripes, lion's spots, zebra's stripes, and lights decoration patterns *(Figures 4.21, 4.22, 4.23, 4.24, 4.25 on pages 219 to 223)* on transparencies.

10. Cut just to the inside of dotted lines on each animal transparency.

11. Cut out lights decoration transparency and color "light bulbs" with permanent markers.

12. Attach a magnetic strip to the back of each piece, hiding magnetic strip when possible on all transparencies.

(see Figures 4.15, 4.16, 4.17, 4.18, 4.19, 4.20, 4.21, 4.22, 4.23, 4.24, 4.25 on pages 213 to 223)

Halloween Countdown

Ten candy corns—yellow, orange, and white.
(Count while placing candy corns on flannel board.)
Nine chocolate kisses to last all night.
(Count while placing kisses on flannel board.)
Eight lollipops—I'll have them for a snack.
(Count while placing lollipops on flannel board.)
Seven jellybeans—my favorite color is black.
(Count while placing jellybeans on flannel board.)
Six shiny nickels—all round and new.
(Count while placing nickels on flannel board.)
Five candy bars—I'm glad I got a few!
(Count while placing candy bars on flannel board.)
Four candied apples with peanuts on the top.
(Count while placing candied apples on flannel board.)
Three sticks of gum at the last stop.
(Count while placing gum on flannel board.)
Two iced cookies—a witch and a ghost.
(Count while placing cookies on flannel board.)
One bag full of treats—I love Halloween the most!
(Place bag on flannel board.)

To Make as a Flannel Story:

1. Cut all patterns from felt in colors of your choice, unless otherwise indicated in story.
2. Enhance with felt markers.

(see Figures 4.26, 4.27, 4.28, 4.29, 4.30, 4.31 on pages 224 to 229)

To Make as a Magnetic Story:

1. Reproduce patterns.
2. Color all patterns in colors of your choice, unless otherwise indicated in story.
3. Laminate patterns.
4. Cut out patterns.
5. Attach a magnetic strip to the back of each piece.

(see Figures 4.26, 4.27, 4.28, 4.29, 4.30, 4.31 on pages 224 to 229)

One Dark and Gloomy Night

(Before beginning, place all five cats at bottom of flannel board. Play number seven from CD.)
One dark and gloomy night,
Five cats wished for a flight,
   (Point to cats or hold up five fingers.)
Just then a magic broom sped by.
Zoom! Zoom!
   (Place broom on flannel board with enough room above it to place cats on broom.)
One jumped onto the broom,
'Cuz there was lots of room,
   (Place one cat on far end of broom.)
Four cats are waiting for a ride.
   (Point to cats or hold up four fingers.)
Meow! Meow!
One dark and gloomy night,
Four cats wished for a flight,
   (Point to cats or hold up four fingers.)
Just then a magic broom sped by.
Zoom! Zoom!
   (Point to broom.)
One jumped onto the broom,
'Cuz there was lots of room,
   (Place second cat on broom next to first cat.)
Three cats are waiting for a ride.
   (Point to cats or hold up three fingers.)
Meow! Meow!
One dark and gloomy night,
Three cats wished for a flight,
   (Point to cats or hold up three fingers.)
Just then a magic broom sped by.
Zoom! Zoom!
   (Point to broom.)
One jumped onto the broom,
'Cuz there was lots of room,
   (Place third cat on broom next to second cat.)
Two cats are waiting for a ride.
   (Point to cats or hold up two fingers.)
Meow! Meow!
One dark and gloomy night,
Two cats wished for a flight,
   (Point to cats or hold up two fingers.)

Just then a magic broom sped by.

Zoom! Zoom!

(Point to broom.)

One jumped onto the broom,

'Cuz there was lots of room,

(Place fourth cat on broom next to third cat.)

One cat is waiting for a ride.

(Point to cat or hold up one finger.)

Meow! Meow!

One dark and gloomy night,

One cat wished for a flight,

(Point to cat or hold up one finger.)

Just then a magic broom sped by.

Zoom! Zoom!

(Point to broom.)

He jumped onto the broom,

'Cuz there was lots of room,

(Place fifth cat on broom next to fourth cat.)

No more cats are waiting for a ride.

Meow! Meow!

To Make as a Flannel Story:

1. Cut all patterns from felt colors of your choice.
2. Glue broom felt pieces together matching "A" to "a," "B" to "b," and "C" to "c" as indicated on pattern.
3. Enhance with felt markers.

    NOTE: To stiffen broom handle, spread white glue evenly over reverse side and allow to dry over night.

    (see Figures 4.32, 4.33, 4.34 on pages 230 to 232)

To Make as a Magnetic Story:

1. Reproduce patterns.
2. Color all patterns in colors of your choice.
3. Cut out patterns.
4. Tape broom pieces together, matching "A" to "a," "B" to "b," and "C" to "c" as indicated on pattern.
5. Laminate patterns.
6. Cut out patterns.
7. Attach a magnetic strip to the back of each piece.

    (see Figures 4.32, 4.33, 4.34 on pages 230 to 232)

The Perfect Pet

(This song can be sung to the tune "I'm Bringin' Home a Baby Bumblebee." Before beginning, place the animals on flannel board, from left to right and in the following order: guinea pig, toucan, rabbit, and puppy. Next, place the extra beak on top of the toucan's beak, the extra ears on top of the rabbit's ears, and the extra tail on top of the puppy's tail, so that they each appear to be one.)

I'm walkin' 'round the pet store, lookin' for a pet,
   (Walk in place, then shade eyes with hand, and look around.)
No, I haven't found the one I want yet.
   (Shake head no.)
A guinea pig's fur is just right you see,
   (Point to guinea pig.)
But his nightlife's way too much for me!
   (Yawn.)
Oh—I'm walkin' 'round the pet store, lookin' for a pet,
   (Walk in place, then shade eyes with hand, and look around.)
No, I haven't found the one I want yet.
   (Shake head no.)
A toucan's beak is just right you see,
But his talkin's way too much for me!
   (Make "talking" motion with hand, then remove extra beak, and place it over the guinea pig's mouth.)
Oh—I'm walkin' 'round the pet store, lookin' for a pet,
   (Walk in place, then shade eyes with hand, and look around.)
No, I haven't found the one I want yet.
   (Shake head no.)
A rabbit's ears are just right you see,
But his hoppin's way too much for me!
   (Jump in place, then remove rabbit's extra ears, and place on top of the guinea pig's head.)
Oh—I'm walkin' 'round the pet store, lookin' for a pet,
   (Walk in place, then shade eyes with hand, and look around.)
No, I haven't found the one I want yet.
   (Shake head no.)
A puppy's tail is just right you see,
But his barkin's way too much for me!
   (Cover ears with hands, then remove puppy's extra tail, and place it on the guinea pig's rear end.)
Oh—I'm walkin' 'round the pet store, lookin' for a pet,
   (Walk in place, then shade eyes with hand, and look around.)
No, I haven't found the one I want yet.
   (Shake head no.)
I'm walkin' out the pet store without a pet,
   (Shrug shoulders. If singing, speak the last line:)
Guess the perfect pet hasn't been created yet!

To Make as a Flannel Story:

1. Cut all patterns from felt colors of your choice.
2. Enhance with felt markers.

    (see Figures 4.35, 4.36, 4.37, 4.38, 4.39 on pages 233 to 237)

To Scare Away the Crows

(This song can be sung to the tune of "Do You Know the Muffin Man?")
I started out with a frying pan, took it to the field, what a plan.
   (Wave frying pan then place, handle down, on flannel board.)
I started out with a frying pan to scare away the crows.
   (Lift both hands above head and drop them to thighs.)
I stuck it in a bale of hay, added glue to make it stay.
   (Place hay lengthwise over handle of frying pan and then hold up glue bottle.)
Stuck it in a bale of hay to scare away the crows.
   (Lift both hands above head and drop them to thighs.)
Welded on an old horseshoe, wasn't enough, I needed two.
   (Place one horseshoe and then the other on frying pan to resemble eyes.)
Welded on an old horseshoe to scare away the crows.
   (Lift both hands above head and drop them to thighs.)
Wired on a garden spade, thought the birds would be afraid.
   (Place garden spade, handle up, to resemble nose.)
Wired on a garden spade to scare away the crows.
   (Lift both hands above head and drop them to thighs.)
Poked it with a metal rake, went clean through, what a mistake.
   (Place rake on hay bale.)
Poked it with a metal rake to scare away the crows.
   (Lift both hands above head and drop them to thighs.)
Gathered up a flowerpot, put it here, liked it a lot.
   (Place flowerpot on frying pan to resemble hat.)
Gathered up a flowerpot to scare away the crows.
   (Lift both hands above head and drop them to thighs.)
Time to quit; I'm going inside, looked out the window, full of pride.
   (Walk in place and then pretend to put thumbs behind suspenders.)
Couldn't believe what I spied, at least a million crows!
   (Place window with crows over "scarecrow.")

To Make as a Magnetic Story:

1. Reproduce patterns.
2. Color all patterns in colors of your choice.
3. Cut out patterns.

4. Tape frying pan to handle "A" to "a."
5. Tape rake handle together "B" to "b."
6. Laminate patterns.
7. Cut out patterns.
8. Attach a magnetic strip to the back of each piece.

(see Figures 4.40, 4.41, 4.42, 4.43, 4.44, 4.45 on pages 238 to 243)

OPTIONAL: Use completed "Scarecrow" illustration as a coloring sheet (*Figure 4.45 on page 243*).

To Make Window:

1. Reproduce all four window panes onto transparencies.
2. Tape the four window panes together *(Figure 4.46—top left to Figure 4.47—top right, then Figure 4.48—bottom left to Figure 4.49—bottom right)* creating a large four-paned window. *(see Figure 4.50 on page 248)*

(see Figures 4.46, 4.47, 4.48, 4.49, 4.50 on pages 244 to 248)

Halloween Parade

Station signs, designed for placement at each stop along the parade route, are numbered one through ten. Reproduce paper treats to provide one for each little goblin and be sure to create a sample to display at each stop. Inexpensive candy treats may also be included. Check with a local grocery store; many are willing to provide a treat in exchange for advertisement at your event. Before the parade begins, assign someone to lead the parade. *(Play number eight from CD)* and let the parade begin!

Halloween March

FOUR! THREE! TWO! ONE!
March with us it's lots of fun!
First the left foot, then the right,
This Hall-o-ween par-ade is out of sight!

ONE! TWO! THREE! FOUR!
Look at her-oes we a-dore!
Su-per-man is sure to win,
There's Spid-er-man with his web to spin!

FOUR! THREE! TWO! ONE!
March with us it's lots of fun!
First the left foot, then the right,
This Hall-o-ween par-ade is out of sight!

ONE! TWO! THREE! FOUR!
Cin-der-ell-a sweep that floor!
Fair-y prin-cess sure looks good,
And Slee-ping Beau-ty's with Ro-bin Hood!

FOUR! THREE! TWO! ONE!
March with us it's lots of fun!
First the left foot, then the right,
This Hall-o-ween par-ade is out of sight!

ONE! TWO! THREE! FOUR!
Cow-boys, cow-girls, and much more!
Horses, cows, and old red hens,
All pran-cin' and strut-tin' in se-p'rate pins!

FOUR! THREE! TWO! ONE!
March with us it's lots of fun!
First the left foot, then the right,
This Hall-o-ween par-ade is out of sight!

ONE! TWO! THREE! FOUR!
Roc-ket ships will help them soar!
As-tro-nauts from ou-ter space,
And alien ro-bots keep-in' pace!

FOUR! THREE! TWO! ONE!
March with us it's lots of fun!
First the left foot, then the right,
This Hall-o-ween par-ade is out of sight!

ONE! TWO! THREE! FOUR!
List-en to the li-ons roar!
Ti-gers, bears, a kan-ga-roo,
Big el-e-phants, and ze-bras in the zoo!

FOUR! THREE! TWO! ONE!
March with us it's lots of fun!
First the left foot, then the right,
This Hall-o-ween par-ade is out of sight!

ONE! TWO! THREE! FOUR!
Swim-mers from the o-cean shore!
Crabs and fish-es with blue tails,
Sea-hors-es and there are great big whales!

FOUR! THREE! TWO! ONE!
March with us it's lots of fun!
First the left foot, then the right,
This Hall-o-ween par-ade is out of sight!

ONE! TWO! THREE! FOUR!
An-cient times are sure to score!
Crea-tures with e-nor-mous necks,
Din-o-saurs and Tyr-ann-o-saur-us Rex!

FOUR! THREE! TWO! ONE!
March with us it's lots of fun!
First the left foot, then the right,
This Hall-o-ween par-ade is out of sight!

ONE! TWO! THREE! FOUR!
Fairy tale char-ac-ters ga-lore!
Knights and dra-gons they all came,
Bill-y goats gruff with an og-re to tame!

FOUR! THREE! TWO! ONE!
March with us it's lots of fun!
First the left foot, then the right,
This Hall-o-ween par-ade is out of sight!

ONE! TWO! THREE! FOUR!
Wit-ches go-ing door-to-door!
Scar-y goblins and a ghost,
Spook-y nights are what they like the most!

FOUR! THREE! TWO! ONE!
March with us it's lots of fun!
First the left foot, then the right,
This Hall-o-ween par-ade is out of sight!

ONE! TWO! THREE! FOUR!
Boy my feet are get-tin' sore!
Man-y treats are in my bag,
I'm tryin' to keep up and not lol-ly-gag!

Craft "Treats" for Parade

The following handouts with patterns and instructions for inexpensive treats are provided:

- Bat finger puppet
  (see Figure 4.51 on page 249)
- Bookmarks

  1. "Boo" Bookmark
  (see Figure 4.52 on page 250)
  2. "Happy Halloween" Bookmark
  (see Figure 4.53 on page 251)
  3. "Pumpkin Vine" Bookmark
  (see Figure 4.54 on page 252)
  4. "Scarecrow" Bookmark
  (see Figure 4.55 on page 253)

- Dancing Jack Craft
  (see Figure 4.56 on page 254)
- Halloween Candy Matching Activity
  (see Figure 4.57 on page 255)
- Halloween Cat Mask
  (see Figure 4.58 on page 256)
- Help Baby Boo Find His Mama Maze
  (see Figure 4.59 on page 257)
- Pumpkin Head Craft
  (see Figure 4.60 on page 258)
- Scarecrow Coloring Sheet
  (see Figure 4.61 on page 259)

Halloween Boo Support Materials

Halloween Boo Support Materials run from pages 199 to 259.

Figure 4.1 Publicity Page for "Halloween Boo"

Halloween Boo Station Assignments

Station	Treat	Location	Staff
1	_____	_____	_____
2	_____	_____	_____
3	_____	_____	_____
4	_____	_____	_____
5	_____	_____	_____
6	_____	_____	_____
7	_____	_____	_____
8	_____	_____	_____
9	_____	_____	_____
10	_____	_____	_____

Things to do:

_____

_____

_____

_____

_____

_____

_____

_____

Figure 4.2 "Halloween Boo" Station Assignment Form

Sample Halloween Boo Station Assignments

Station	Treat	Location	Staff
1	Halloween bag	outside/tree	Bonnie
2	Bat finger puppet	inside storytime room	Chris
3	BOOO Bookmark	Young Adult desk	Deena
4	Tootsie roll candy	Volunteer desk	Traci
5	Dancing Jack	Reference desk	Tyler
6	Candy Match-up	Left side of Ref Desk	John
7	Red Vine Candy	Circulation Desk	Kim
8	Cat Mask	Security Office	Ray
9	Scarecrow coloring sheet	Children's Desk	Trisha
10	Punch & Cookies	outside	Gail

Things to do:
- Check with local merchants for cookies, punch, and candy donations or discounts
- check irrigation schedule
- recruit volunteers
- run off all handouts (estimate 300 children)
- pick up coolers for punch and fill with ice
- set up microphones and stereo
- set up tables outside for punch & cookies
- check supply of napkins and cups

Figure 4.3 Sample "Halloween Boo" Station Assignments

Figure 4.4 Certificate for "Halloween Boo"

Figure 4.5 Station Sign for "Halloween Boo"

Figure 4.6 Station Sign for "Halloween Boo"

Figure 4.7 Station Sign for "Halloween Boo"

Figure 4.8 Station Sign for "Halloween Boo"

Figure 4.9 Station Sign for "Halloween Boo"

Figure 4.10 Station Sign for "Halloween Boo"

Figure 4.11 Station Sign for "Halloween Boo"

Figure 4.12 Station Sign for "Halloween Boo"

Figure 4.13 Station Sign for "Halloween Boo"

Figure 4.14 Station Sign for "Halloween Boo"

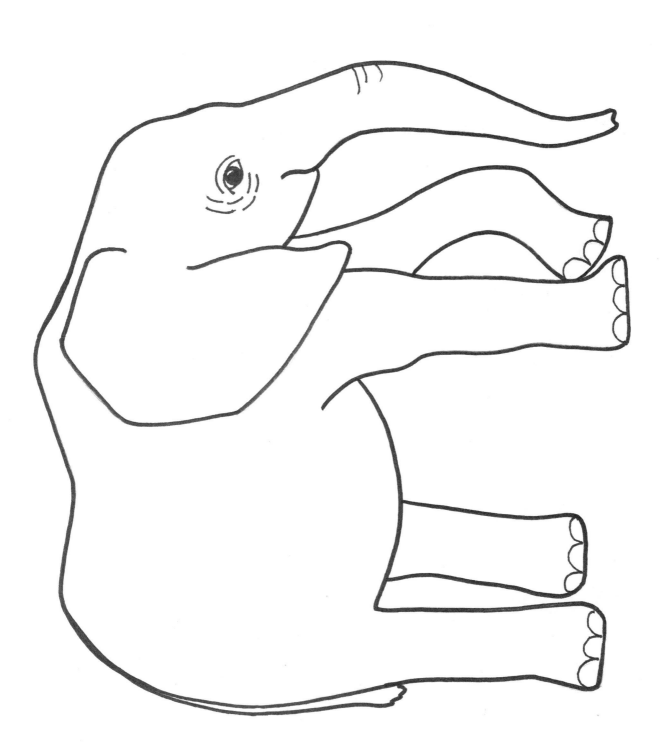

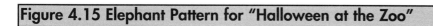

Figure 4.15 Elephant Pattern for "Halloween at the Zoo"

Figure 4.16 Giraffe Pattern for "Halloween at the Zoo"

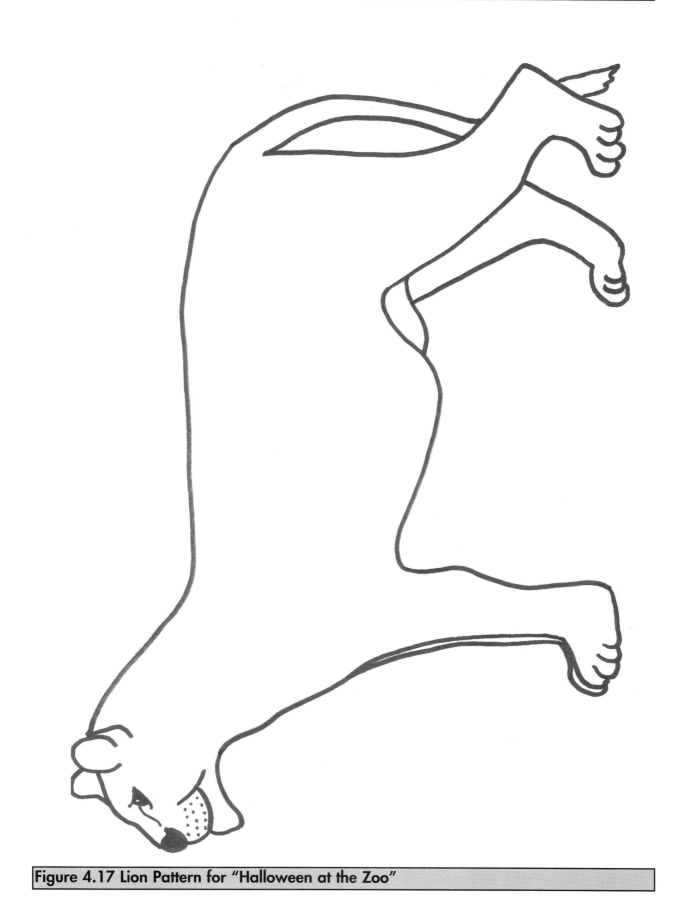

Figure 4.17 Lion Pattern for "Halloween at the Zoo"

Figure 4.18 Zebra Pattern for "Halloween at the Zoo"

Lion's Mane

Zebra's Mane

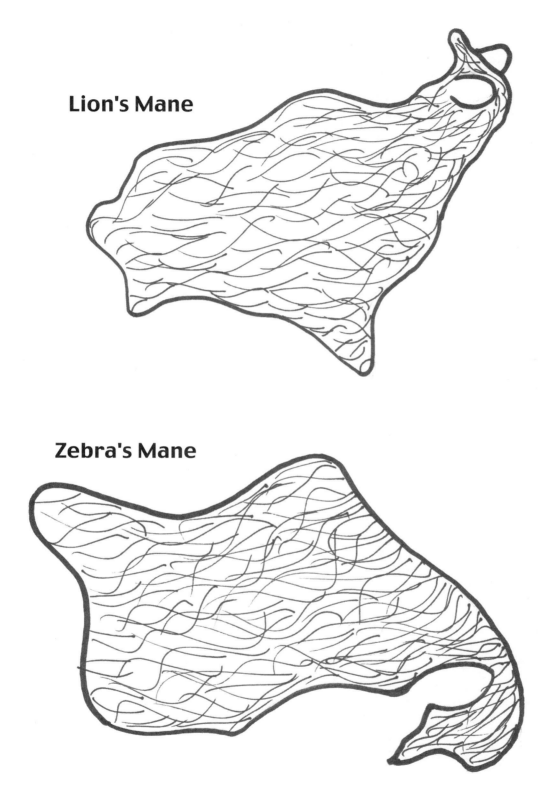

Figure 4.19 Lion's and Zebra's Mane Patterns for "Halloween at the Zoo"

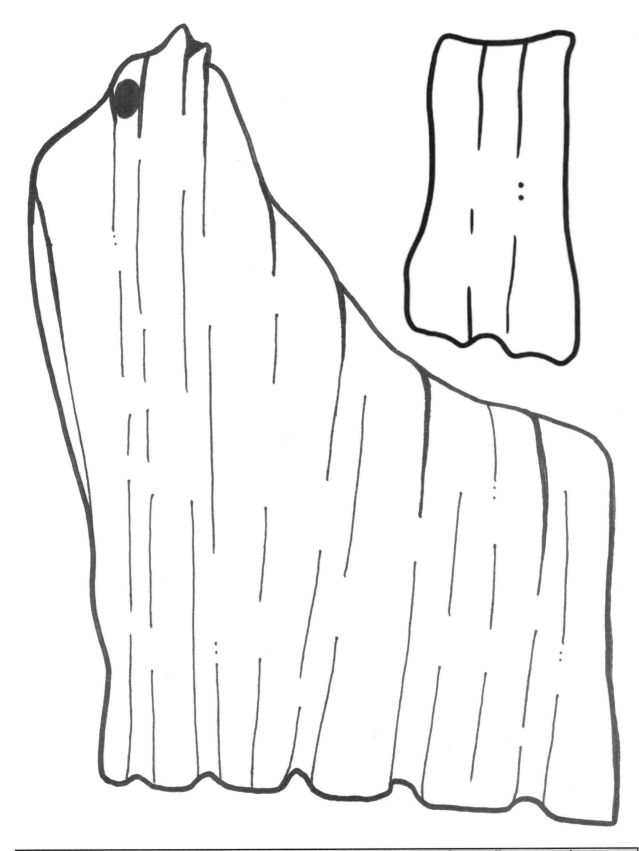

Figure 4.20 Giraffe's Ghost Costume and Elephant's Towel Patterns for "Halloween at the Zoo"

Figure 4.21 Giraffe Transparency Pattern for "Halloween at the Zoo"

Figure 4.22 Elephant Transparency Pattern for "Halloween at the Zoo"

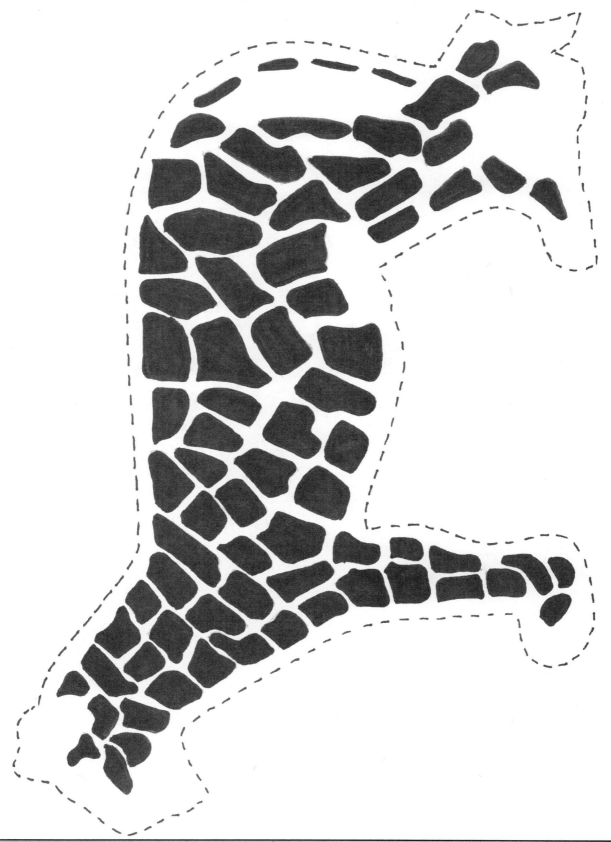

Figure 4.23 Lion Transparency Pattern for "Halloween at the Zoo"

Figure 4.24 Zebra Transparency Pattern for "Halloween at the Zoo"

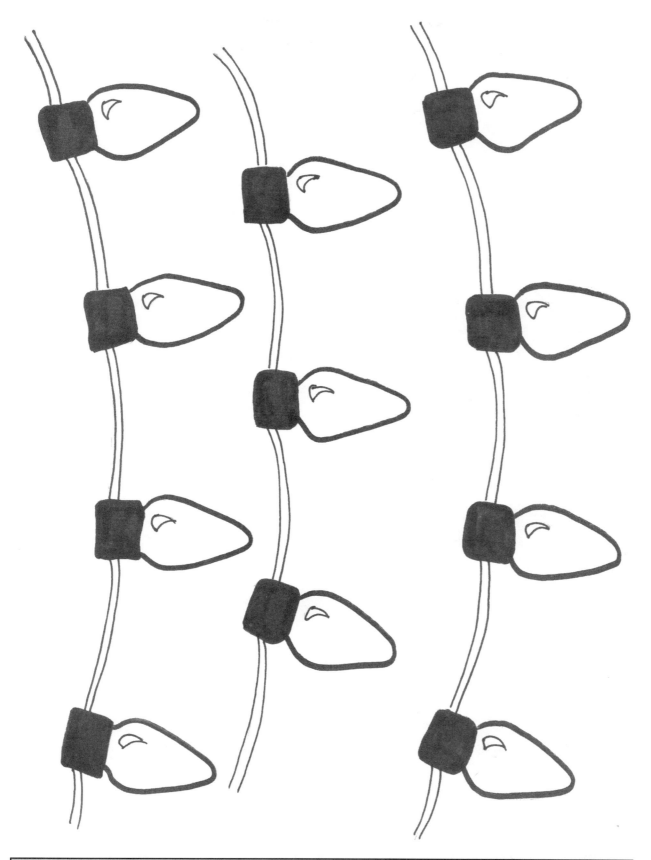

Figure 4.25 Lights Decoration Transparency Pattern for "Halloween at the Zoo"

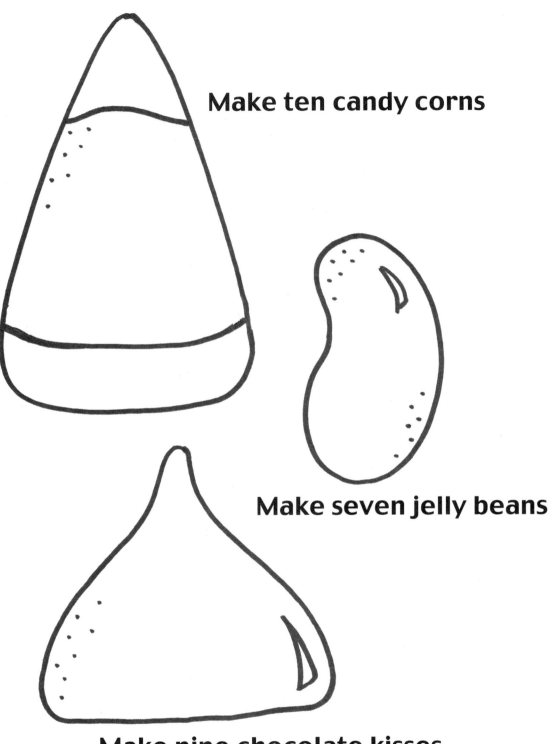

Make ten candy corns

Make seven jelly beans

Make nine chocolate kisses

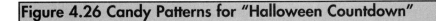

Figure 4.26 Candy Patterns for "Halloween Countdown"

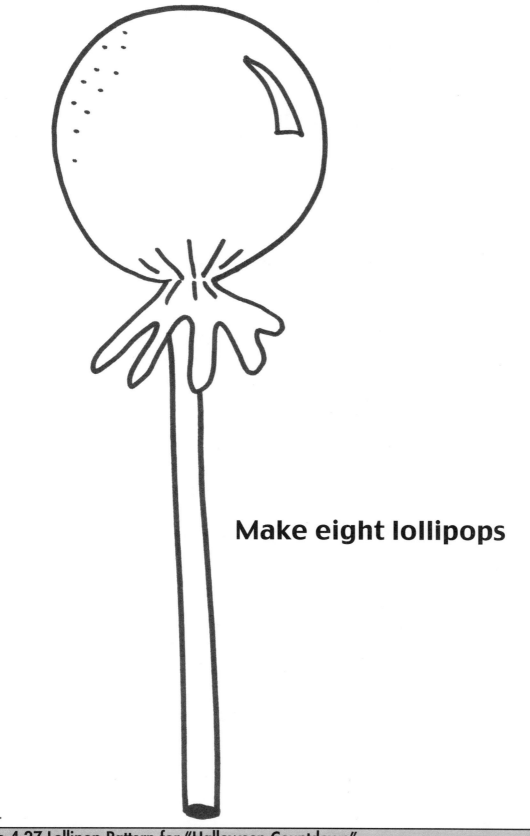

Make eight lollipops

Figure 4.27 Lollipop Pattern for "Halloween Countdown"

Make four candied apples

Figure 4.28 Candied Apple Pattern for "Halloween Countdown"

Make six shiny nickels

Make five candy bars

Make three sticks of gum

Figure 4.29 Patterns for "Halloween Countdown"

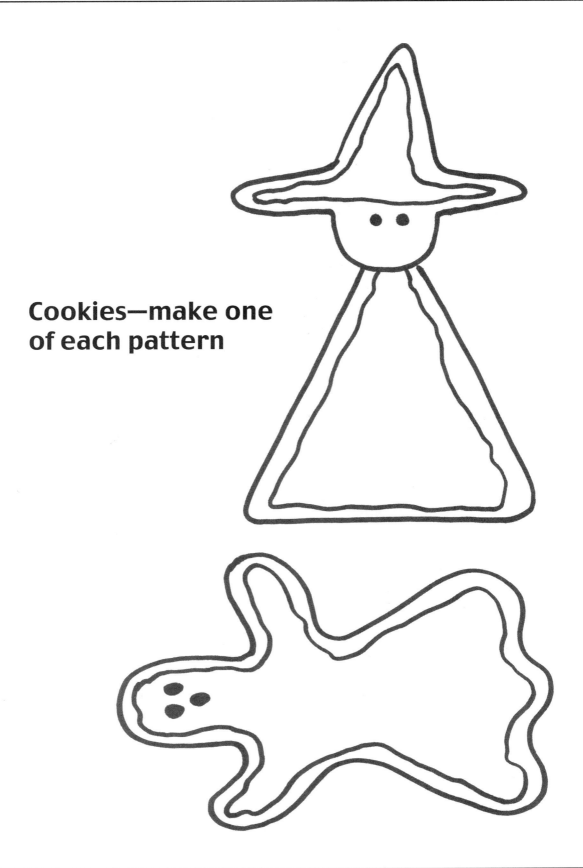

Cookies—make one of each pattern

Figure 4.30 Cookie Patterns for "Halloween Countdown"

Make one bag

Figure 4.31 Trick or Treat Bag Pattern for "Halloween Countdown"

Make five cats

Figure 4.32 Cat Pattern for "One Dark and Gloomy Night"

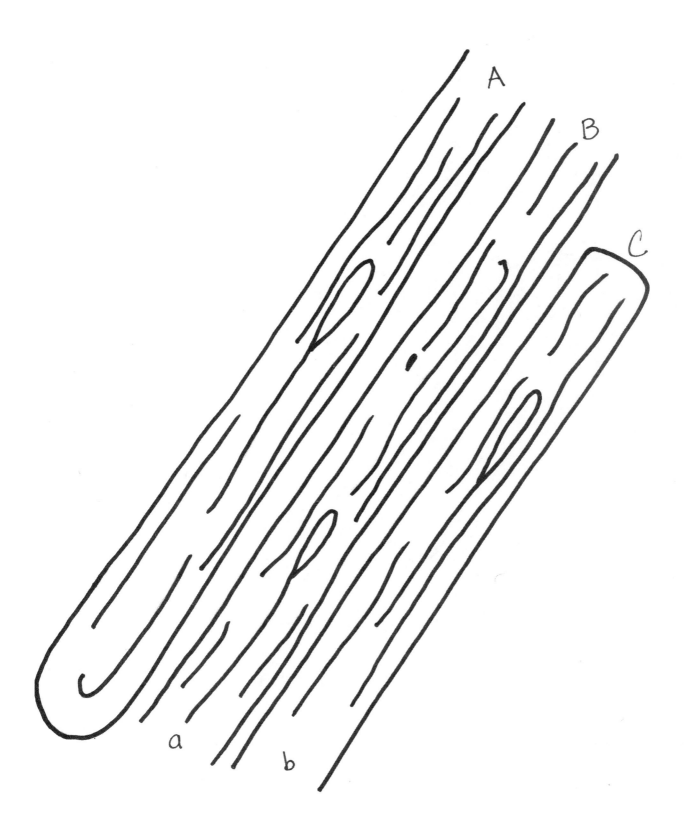

Figure 4.33 Broom Pattern for "One Dark and Gloomy Night"

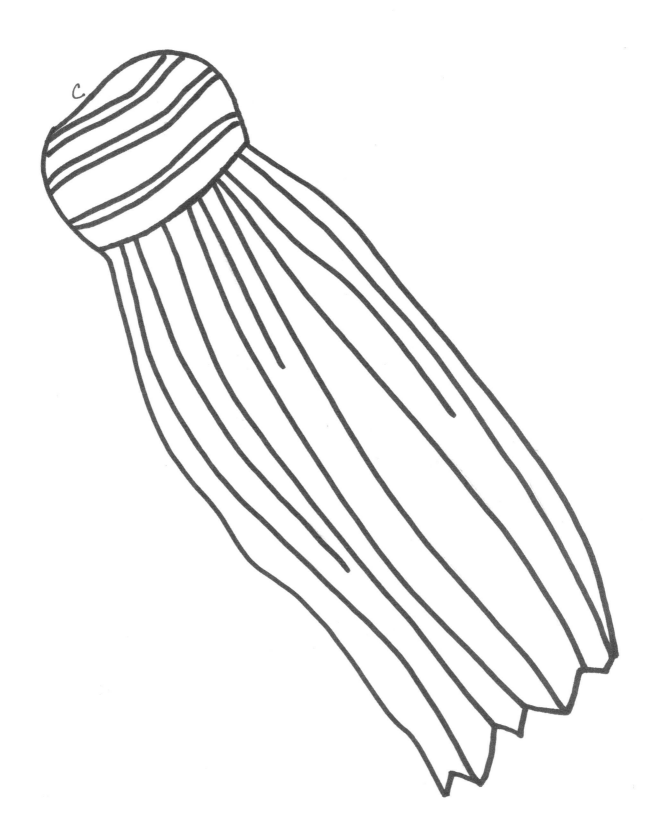

Figure 4.34 Broom Pattern for "One Dark and Gloomy Night"

Figure 4.35 Guinea Pig Pattern for "The Perfect Pet"

Figure 4.36 Toucan Pattern for "The Perfect Pet"

Figure 4.37 Rabbit Pattern for "The Perfect Pet"

Figure 4.38 Puppy Pattern for "The Perfect Pet"

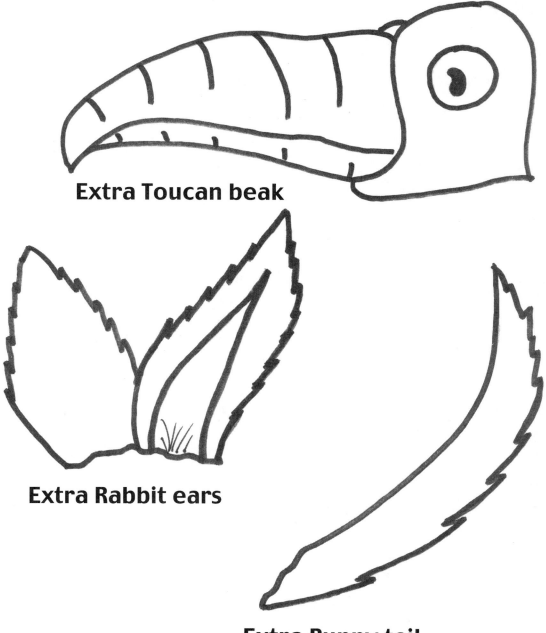

Extra Toucan beak

Extra Rabbit ears

Extra Puppy tail

Figure 4.39 Patterns for "The Perfect Pet"

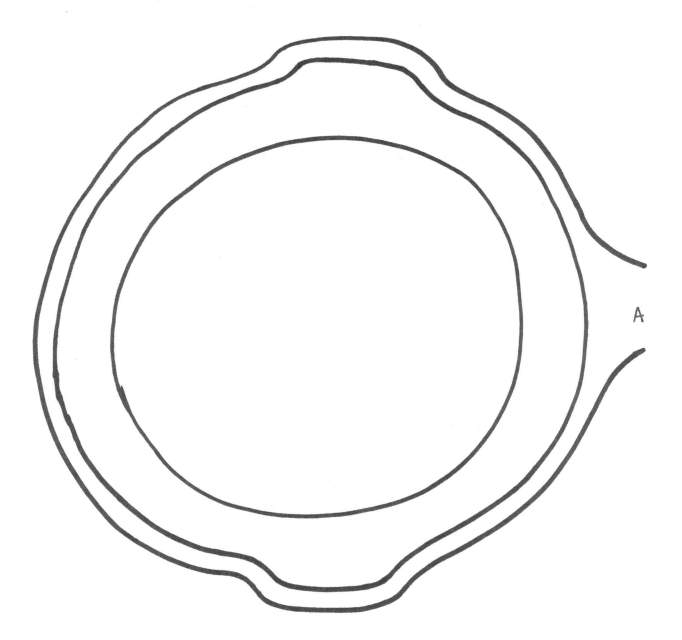

A

Figure 4.40 Frying Pan Pattern for "To Scare Away the Crows"

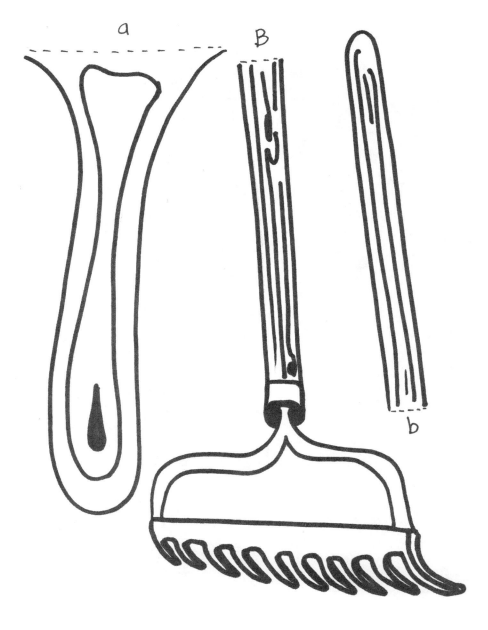

Figure 4.41 Frying Pan Handle and Rake Patterns for "To Scare Away the Crows"

Figure 4.42 Bale of Hay Pattern for "To Scare Away the Crows"

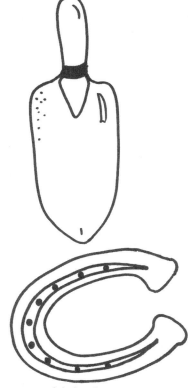

Make two

Figure 4.43 Garden Spade and Horseshoe Patterns for "To Scare Away the Crows"

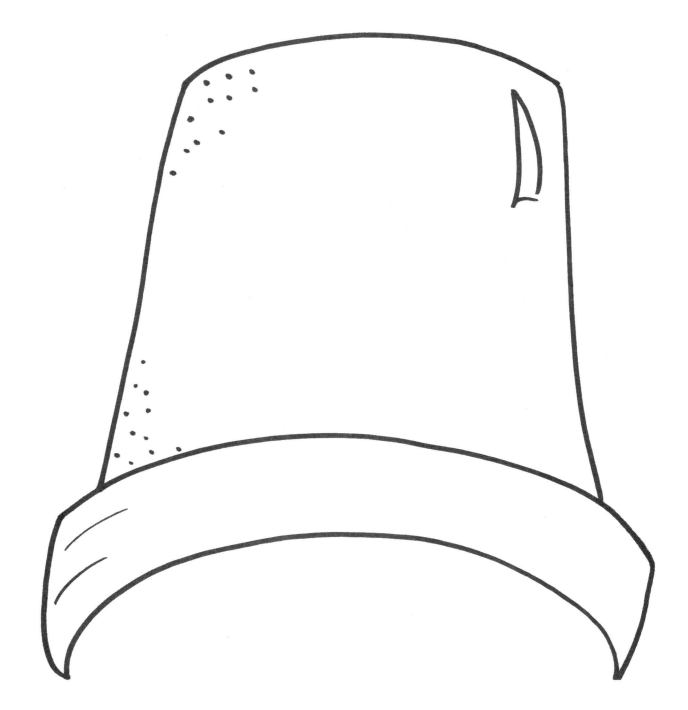

Figure 4.44 Flowerpot Pattern for "To Scare Away the Crows"

Figure 4.45 Coloring Sheet for Completed "To Scare Away the Crows"

Figure 4.46 Top Left Window Pane Pattern for "To Scare Away the Crows"

Figure 4.47 Top Right Window Pane Pattern for "To Scare Away the Crows"

Figure 4.48 Bottom Left Window Pane Pattern for "To Scare Away the Crows"

Figure 4.49 Bottom Right Window Pane Pattern for "To Scare Away the Crows"

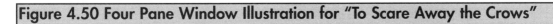

Figure 4.50 Four Pane Window Illustration for "To Scare Away the Crows"

To make bat finger puppet:
  1. cut out bats
  2. glue together around edges—only stopping at X's
  3. insert index finger into opening between X's

Figure 4.51 Bat Finger Puppet Pattern

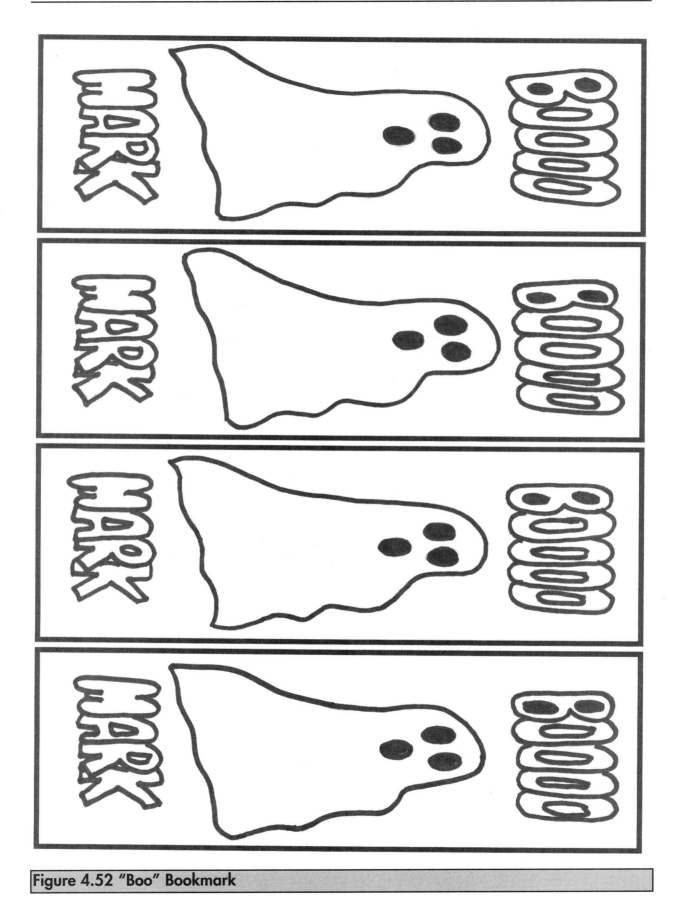

Figure 4.52 "Boo" Bookmark

Figure 4.53 "Happy Halloween" Bookmark

Figure 4.54 "Pumpkin Vine" Bookmark

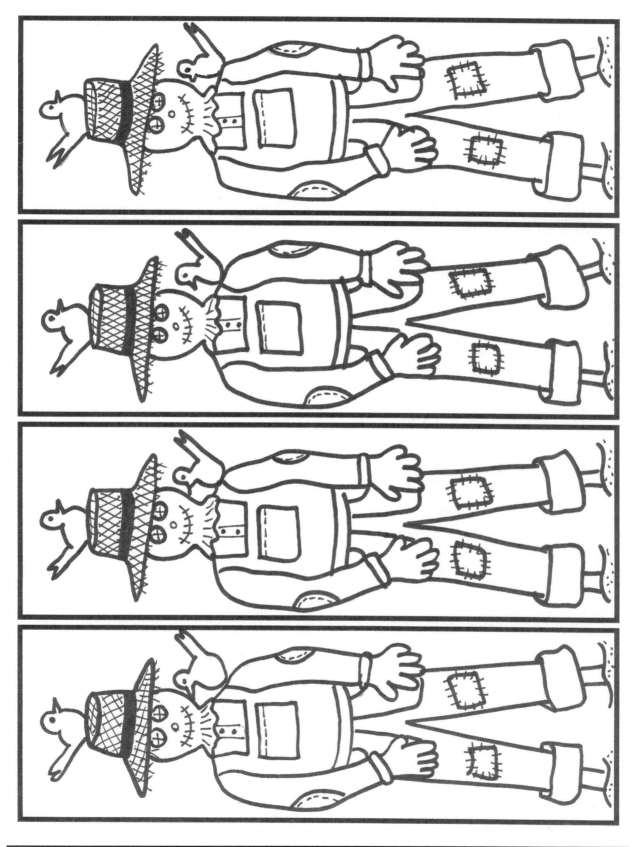

Figure 4.55 "Scarecrow" Bookmark

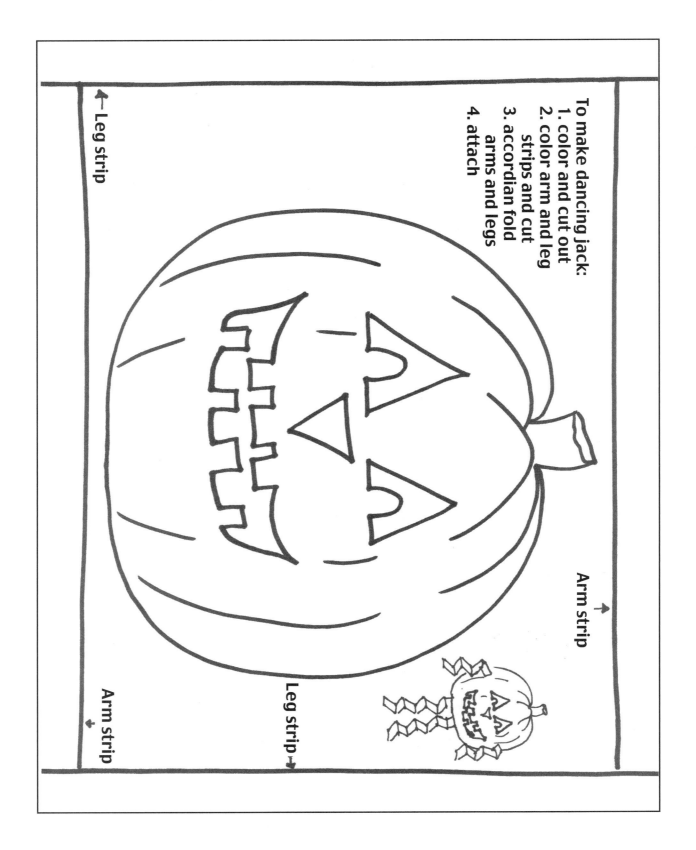

To make dancing jack:
1. color and cut out
2. color arm and leg strips and cut
3. accordian fold arms and legs
4. attach

← Leg strip

Arm strip →

Leg strip →

Arm strip ←

Figure 4.56 Pattern for "Dancing Jack Craft"

Draw a line to match the candy.

Figure 4.57 Halloween Candy Matching Activity

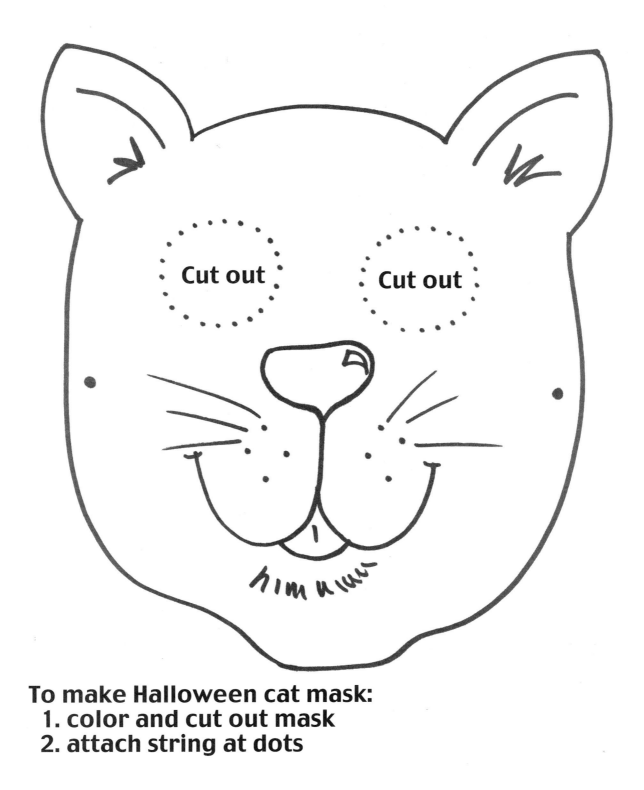

To make Halloween cat mask:
 1. color and cut out mask
 2. attach string at dots

Figure 4.58 Halloween Cat Mask

Figure 4.59 Help Baby Boo Find His Mama Maze

To make pumpkin head:
1. color and cut out pumpkin
2. glue yellow cellophane behind eyes, nose, and mouth
3. hang in window

Figure 4.60 Pumpkin Head Craft

Figure 4.61 Scarecrow Coloring Sheet

Index

About the Authors

Gail Benton (left) and Trisha Waichulaitis (right), authors of *Ready-to-Go Storytimes*, continue to work together creating successful children's stories and programs. During the past thirteen years they have presented at state and national library conferences and conducted continuing education workshops for teachers, librarians, daycare providers, and home-school parents. They are both children's librarians at the City of Mesa Library, where they enjoy sharing their stories and songs with Mesa's youngest patrons.